Outlive
THE LABELS

Volume III
From Breakdowns to Breakthroughs

VISIONARY
#1 INTERNATIONAL BEST-SELLING AUTHOR
MARY KAYE HOLMES
+17 Thought Leaders and Overcomers

JOAN JAMES PUBLISHING ISLAND

Outlive the Labels Volume III
From Breakdowns to Breakthroughs
ISBN 978-1-5136-8908-1

Joan James Publishing Island
Waterbury, CT 06704
Printed in the United States of America

TABLE OF CONTENTS

When Breakdowns Become Breakthroughs

Mary Kaye Holmes

*B*reakdowns can come in many forms: emotional, physical, spiritual, relational, financial, social, situational, etc. When something or someone experiences a breakdown there is a deterioration, a failure, or a malfunction. When a person goes through an emotional breakdown, they can feel like all hope is lost and they don't see a way out of the downward spiral they've found themselves in. Their life may feel as if it is spinning out of control and as if they are on an emotional rollercoaster – a rollercoaster that has gone off the rails and all they can do is hold on until it's over and it culminates in a loud, booming CRASH! I've been there. The co-authors of this book have been there. We write our stories to let you know that you are not alone.

Outlive the Labels Volume III: From Breakdowns to Breakthroughs, is a collection of stories that remind us that we rise by lifting others. Powerful thought-leaders and overcomers joined forces to inspire, motivate and empower you for positive change. The transparent narratives that you will read will grip your heart and move you to compassion for the plight of the writers, but it will ultimately produce hope and encouragement and send the message that no matter your situation or circumstance, there is life beyond the labels.

You will read stories like Dianne Brown's where she writes passionately about her son's journey of not only being born blind and deaf, but born with a cleft face, palate and head as well. You will discover how her son's life not only changed her, but saved a marriage as well. Outlive the Labels Volume III will breathe new levels of hope and inspiration into you with stories of surviving domestic abuse like Laticka Weaver-Smith and Shalonda Chaney-White, stories of overcoming generational labeling like that of Alison Jaye, and discovering our purpose in moments of great pain like the story of Liliana Marie. You will also read stories about overcoming incarceration, financial setbacks, and sexual abuse – all of these real life issues are covered in riveting detail, but most importantly, they contain a common thread that you will not only survive, but thrive beyond trauma.

Allow these narratives to motivate you to take charge and create change in your own life, and move you to forgive those who have overlooked you, mistreated you and abused you. Forgive those who have looked down on you, neglected you and abandoned you. It is imperative that we remember the past, not as a source of contention and bitterness, but as a stark reminder to not repeat it or continue a perpetual cycle of harm. We've heard the phrase "hurt people, hurt people". However, hurt people also help people. We understand the low place, we understand the pain, and we understand the resentment one can feel from constantly being left behind to suffer in silence. But, we also understand that all things work together for the good, and every situation that happened didn't happen *to* us, but it happened *for* us. We survived so that we can reach back and pull someone else out of the pit. We are here and now we are also heard. These are the stories of survivors. Thank you for supporting our mission of outliving every label.

—Mary Kaye Holmes, Visionary of Outlive the Labels
Volumes I, III, and III

❧

Mary Kaye Holmes

As a #1 International Best-Selling Author, public speaker, and Certified Life & Success Coach, Dr. Mary Kaye Holmes is living out her assignment to empower everyone she encounters. She is the award-winning founder of the global movement "Outlive the Labels" and a mouthpiece for criminal justice reform and human trafficking awareness. As a survivor of human trafficking, domestic violence and incarceration, she is a sought-after trusted authority on thriving beyond adversity and speaks from her heart concerning real issues that plague women from all walks of life. Her memoir, *Trapped in Plain Sight: The Unfamiliar Face of Human Trafficking* was recently released June 2021 and achieved best-seller status on Amazon.

Dr. Mary Kaye's latest endeavor is her new 501(c)3, the H.A.L.O. Campaign (Human Trafficking Advocacy and Learning Opportunities for Exploited Black and Brown Girls), to create pathways to employment and entrepreneurship for human trafficking survivors. As a part of this initiative, she recently founded the Shirley Rose Tailoring Academy for human trafficking and gender-based violence survivors in Malawi, Africa.

Dr. Mary Kaye is a graduate of New York Law School and currently serves as In-House Corporate Counsel for a NYC financial services firm.

Please follow Mary Kaye on all social media platforms @hearmaryspeak

You may also visit her website marykayeholmes.com

"I AM..."
Author Unknown

Me: Hey, God.

God: Hello, my love.

Me: I'm falling apart. Can you put me back together?

God: I would rather not.

Me: ☹

God: Because you are not a puzzle.

Me: What about all of the pieces of my life that are falling down onto the ground?

God: Let them stay there for a while. They fell off for a reason. Take some time and decide if you need any of those pieces back.

Me: You don't understand! I'm breaking down!

God: No - you don't understand. You are breaking through. What you are feeling is just growing pains. You are shedding the things and the people in your life that are holding you back. You are not falling apart. You are falling into place. Relax. Take some deep breaths and allow those things you don't need any more to fall off of you. Quit holding onto the pieces that don't fit you anymore. Let them fall off. Let them go.

Me: Once I start doing that, what will be left of me?

God: Only the very best pieces of you.

Me: I'm scared of changing.

God: I keep telling you - YOU ARE NOT CHANGING! YOU ARE BECOMING!

Me: Becoming who?

God: Becoming who I created you to be! A person of light and love and charity and hope and courage and joy and mercy and grace and compassion. I made you for more than the shallow pieces you have decided to adorn yourself with that you cling to with such greed and fear. Let those things fall off of you. I love you! Don't change! Become! Become! Become! Become who I made you to be. I'm going to keep telling you this until you remember it.

Me: There goes another piece.

God: Yep. Let it be.

Me: So...I'm not broken?

God: No - but you are breaking like the dawn. It's a new day. Become!! Become!!

Daniel's Gift

Dianne B. Brown

*M*ercy is described as a condescending love, reaching out to meet a need without considering the merit of the person who receives the aid. This reminds me of God's mercy throughout the events surrounding the birth of my son, Daniel. During my emergency C-section, he was born blind, deaf, with a cleft face, palate and head. He had a brain stem but no lobes, only fluid where his brain should be. The technical term is A-lobar-holoprosencephaly. I had died during the procedure and my family was called in. By divine intervention I lived.

When I awoke my mother was at the end of my bed praying for me. It took me a few days to get oriented and realize that I had delivered my newborn. The medical staff did not tell me that I had given birth, because they expected him to die within the first few hours and then days of his life. He did not. The doctors shared that they did not know how he was breathing on his own, but he was. The pediatrician, neurologist and another specialist shared that they believed he would only live one week or two weeks at most. Despite their depressing prognosis and label, Daniel struggled to survive.

The physicians then provided my husband and me information so that we could make the appropriate decisions concerning our newborn, baby Brown's life. My husband wanted to place him in an institution or leave him in the hospital to die. As someone said, "It's the socially acceptable and respectable thing to do." I felt this wasn't an option I would be able to live with. As a believer, my decision would be based on God's will and Word and not on what society dictates. It just seemed right to bring him home and let him spend what time he had left with loved ones. After two weeks of pleading with the head doctor, I was given a pass to take my newborn home for one hour. That hour turned into almost a week before Daniel went into crisis and was readmitted into the hospital.

Again, he was expected to live only a few days. I remember the shock when I was gently told to enjoy him for the brief time we would spend together, as if it were yesterday. During this time, the Lord comforted me through the Word and gave me strength for the days to come. I was keenly aware that we were now walking through the valley of the shadow of death. It was only through God's mercy and a series of events that only the Lord could have orchestrated that Daniel's life was sustained once again. "Who comforts us…that we may be able to comfort them which are in any trouble…"

It was during one of my lowest days, that a young lady

I had never seen before asked to speak to me. Being curious, because I had never seen her on the pediatric unit before, I agreed. Shortly after, I placed my baby back in the crib and we met outside the unit in the hallway. She and her husband had been life flighted in from North Carolina because he was injured in a helicopter crash. He was down the hallway on the burn unit with burns covering over 75 percent of his body. She then confided that she was planning on leaving her husband because she did not think she could love him anymore. This was due to the burns disfiguring him and the painful trauma of the repeated debridement or cleaning treatments she watched her husband endure, to decrease the risk of infection. Then she said, "I don't know if you noticed, but I've been watching you. I've never seen your husband, but I see the love you have for your baby is real. You treat him gently, even though he's not beautiful to look at." I responded compassionately, as I affirmed my love for my child. I said, "Genuine love does not look at what it sees outwardly. It goes deeper and looks at the heart."

I let her know that it was God that has given me grace to go through this experience one day at a time. He will also give you strength if you will allow Him to. She then shared, "I think I can love my husband now because of the love and acceptance you give Daniel." I encouraged her to find one good quality in her husband and something special they enjoyed together and talk about it as she encourages him to get better. By the way she described her husband, I became aware that he was depressed. She shared that she was fearful and upset because he wanted to fly again. The doctors had said that it was unlikely that he would fly in the near future.

I understood that she was afraid of losing him. I was walking in the same shoes, only my situation was with my son. I let her know that I would be praying for them and shared for her to encourage him to pursue flying again. After all, this was a goal he had set and was why he wanted to heal. I was amazed at the way God allowed me to be in the hospital at the time someone needed to receive compassion, comfort, and encouragement. I never imagined that He could use my circumstance of crisis to minister to someone else.

I had totally forgotten about this incident until nine months later when I received a letter in the mail. She shared that she had overcome her fear. Her husband was once again flying, only airplanes this time. She went on to share that their experience strengthened their love for each other and their appreciation of life. In addition, due to the treatment there was hardly any scarring left on his body. Imagine, she thanked *me*! I thanked the Lord for answering my prayers. I also had another reason to be thankful. God had spared Daniel's life once again. Our breakthrough came when he did not pass away as expected and was able to come home. Yes, he was alive, and the Lord showed himself faithful in walking with us through the initial leg of this difficulty and beyond.

Many Christians try to avoid adversity, but I have learned that it is through suffering I have come to know and depend on the Lord each day. Through numerous surgeries, medical procedures and years of therapy today Daniel is a 35-year-old active young man who loves God. He is quick to pray for someone when they ask. Although he continues to have medical challenges, we have outlived the label that he would only live for a few days, weeks and months. We have been blessed with family, friends, church leaders, doctors, nurses, therapists, and other professionals that are believers who prayed, encouraged, and strengthened us along the way.

"Beloved, think it not strange concerning the fiery trial which is to try you, as though some strange thing happened unto you; but rejoice in as much as you are partakers of Christ's sufferings that when His glory shall be revealed, you may be glad with exceeding joy" 1 Peter 4:12-13. Someone may come along who still needs to hear words of comfort. It's in those times that you find your greatest strength, and are able to help encourage someone else while you are pain.

🌿

Dianne Brown

Dianne Brown is a compassionate mother, Ordained Minister, Certified Life Coach, Licensed Mental Health Counselor, and Public Speaker. She is a forward thinker and is known for teaching others to lead by example. She wanted to find a way for her son with special needs to share God's love in the community. Dianne, Daniel and her college friend, Dr. Wylene Reed, began doing outreach, culminating into Daniel's Gift, Inc. [501(c)(3)] over 16 years ago. Minister Brown's passion is to offer hope to individuals, groups and leaders using God's Word through counseling, coaching, Bible study, workshops, and public speaking. She is a world-wide traveler including Africa, Guatemala, Ukraine, the Panama Canal, and the United States since 1990, preaching, educating, and ministering to groups at conferences.

Dianne is a graduate of Reformed Theological Seminary with a Master's of Counseling and The University of Florida with a Bachelor of Science in Communication. You can contact her at therapy@diannebrown.live.

Overcomer

Torree Munson

*T*he old saying, "Look where the Lord brought me from" is a common phrase we say in the church, but it is also my living testimony. I'm an accomplished woman, I must say. Remember, everyone's accomplishments are not the same; they are measured according to the individual. I am on my third marriage (God revealed to me that my husband is my soul mate), an ordained elder, and a mother of four. I have my own business, and I have become an established author, podcaster, life coach, and motivational speaker in ministry that God gave me to steward over.

I tried to commit suicide, but survived. I outlived two abusive relationships, was homeless, but always had a place to lay my head and never starved. I had numerous abortions, and lived to talk about it. I suffered from ailments in my body that stagnated me and kept me bound mentally and physically. I co-pastored a church, but trials and tribulations led me back to sin. Now, I can genuinely say that I am an overcomer! My reputation has been slandered and defamed by my closest friends and relatives. However, by God's Grace, I am still winning!

Breaking Through

I look back and glean over the years of me being a child. The most tender years of my life were looking at things, having dreams, and desiring to be all I could be – not knowing that there were life-changing moments already planted in my subconscious mind that I had no clue about until I became older. People called me spoiled, fat, selfish, weak, gullible, stuck up, insecure, preacher's kid, fast, copycat, and the list can go on. These are all negative labels and I knew I didn't want to be labeled.

We restrict our potential by keeping ourselves confined to negative labels. It is a self-fulfilling prophecy if you believe that you are not good enough, not capable of executing or being all that you can be; if you believe these things, this is what will manifest in your life. I believe we allow others to dictate adverse outcomes in our life, but we feed that to our minds as well. We rehearse that which is false and start believing that which is not valid; it is an illusion and a word curse brought upon us. You feel frustrated and unhappy not knowing that your thoughts play a significant role in your emotions. Not sure if you know, but this causes all kinds of ailments in our body, such as migraines, anxiety, stomach aches, and nausea, which will ultimately cause depression.

The first thing I had to do was forgive myself for not loving myself and looking for love in all the wrong places. This was very hard, but I was determined to move forward and outlive all the labels spoken over my life. Forgiving is critical, and not everyone is willing and ready to unveil themselves, be honest about what they think or feel about themselves, open up, and tell what people have said or done to them. I told myself, *"Torree, I forgive you for allowing yourself to be mistreated by men. Torree, I forgive you for wanting to fit in and not knowing your identity."* Yes, this is what I had to do. I had to excuse myself so that I could free myself from all the mistakes that I made. Yes, name every single one of them. Take your time and write it out and don't worry how long it will take; this is so important for your future. You know that forgiving is never for the other person, but you must be free to move on no matter what the other individual does.

Deliverance played a significant role in me outliving labels. I had to get delivered from that which had me bound due to the doors that I had opened. Now, if the situation happened when you were a child and you were vulnerable and taken advantage of, you still need to be delivered from that which has you bound. You have to denounce and renounce it and take your life back! I know this might sound crazy, but it is the truth. Letting go of what was or is attached to you, which is the very thing that had or has you bound, is very important. The very spirit that has you bound will allow you to become very toxic, despondent, and maybe your behavior will not be tolerable. You have to make a choice to become disciplined and intentional – this is very significant in becoming your true self. I have to reprogram evil thoughts, habits, and behaviors with new affirmations, readings, studying, being around positive people, and new attitude. The brain is the most significant muscle, and if you want it to grow, you have to use and reprogram the bad stuff with good healthy stuff; the knowledge, that is. Have you ever heard the saying "you are what you eat and who you are around?" Exactly; you might have to change your circle of friends to outlive the labels.

Prayer sealed all of this for me. I must say that prayer stabilized me. Prayer is the vehicle I still use today to guide me and to keep me grounded and centered. Prayer is what kept me focused on the goal of outliving the labels. God showed me how to do it, and he gave me peace through the dark storms of infidelity, false accusations, being laughed at, divorced, given a venereal disease in my second marriage, having guns removed from my house, abused, and almost having a mental breakdown. The comfort he gave me was unmeasurable. Only God and prayer are what got me through.

Lessons Learned

I had to continue telling myself that I am an overcomer, I am the righteousness of Christ, I am above and not beneath, I am a lender and not a borrower, I am renewed, revived, refreshed, forgiven, and God loves me – because there were different times in my life when I didn't believe it. This was mandatory; I had to believe something that I didn't see, I had to create my happiness in thought first, and I had to thank God for the manifestation. So, for me I learned that you have control of your thoughts; you control what you do and how you live. Peace is something that you have to fight for ultimately, and it doesn't come easy. The key to your peace and serenity is limiting and separating from the individuals who cause drama and pain. I don't care who the individuals are, if they are not in some way motivating, empowering, helping, coaching, praying, or speaking life into you then baby they are not helping, and they are not for you. Be careful of those that cannot uplift you but always have negative things to say about you, or someone else. If they are gossiping about someone else to you the reality is that is a part of them, and they will gossip about you too. It is time to start discerning the spirit of individuals and make your exit. Not all that say they love the Lord, and a disciple will be who they say they are, they will serve and worship and support you then come with a knife in your back. So, monitoring and setting healthy boundaries is vital, and remembering who you are. Listen, you are loved! Just note, everyone that looks like they are rooting for you is for you. Not everyone that says they love you and want the best for you do. You have to guard your heart and stay focused on the goal, vision, and mandate that God the Father has given you and still love, leave your heart open for agape love. Listen, distractions are coming from every angle, but ultimately you have the power to overcome any obstacles that come in your way. You can become. That is the power that God placed inside of you when you were born. God places everything inside of you that you will need on your life journey, but it's up to you to cultivate, build, and expand what God has given you.

Hope and Inspiration

If you are still breathing, there is still life to become. Breath in your body means that there has been an extension on your life for a purpose to be fulfilled. Don't allow purpose to drift away with the wind and settle on a place called the grave. The grave is full of dreams, mandates, and visions that has not been fulfilled because of stagnation, distractions, unforgiveness, loneliness and many other reasons. Exhaust every resource that God places in front of you and die empty.

🌿

Torree Munson

Torree Munson is a woman that has an excellent testimony for millions of people. An Elder in the church, mother, wife, author, Life Coach, motivational speaker, model, entrepreneur, trendsetter, and a world changer are a few ways to describe her. She is from St. Louis, MO, and lived most of her life in New York City. She has four beautiful children and is happily married to Dr. Munson.

She is the CEO of Torree Munson Ministries, Singles Standing Strong, Divorced but Not Destroyed, and Prosperous Moss's owner. She has completed her first book called Singles Standing Strong and co-authored My Pink Stilettos. This year she launched her Podcast called "Everyday Life with Torree Munson", and has graced several magazines and platforms.

Torree will continue to blaze a trail for the kingdom and set new trends as the Lord gives her the wisdom to do so. To book for engagements, seminars, or one on one coaching sessions, email transparenttorree@gmail.com or you can contact her website www.torreemunson.com

Breaking Every Barrier

Jasmine Spencer

*I*t was the last time I will be in this place that once was home to my 11-year-old daughter and myself. I just had to take one more look. The place was as empty now as when I first purchased it four years ago. After a few deep breaths and surprisingly no tears, I exit for the last time, placing my keys in the mailbox for the bank representative to retrieve. I couldn't even wrap my head around how I got here. Life seemed to be moving along just fine and then I walked off a cliff at the end of the yellow brick road I was on.

The fall seemed to go on forever, and then finally I hit the bottom. Dazed and confused as to what happened, I couldn't help but feel my life was over, and I would never recover. I was looking up from the bottom of a pit and didn't have the strength to figure how to get out. Now, I know, it sounds a little dramatic now, but that's how I felt at the time. I mean who has to face a job layoff, the breakup of a relationship and foreclosure all at the same time!! One of these is depressing enough, but all three can send you spiraling. I felt like I was suffocating, and would have to go outside often just to catch my breath. My daughter was depending on me, so I had to keep moving or at least look like I was moving. To make matters worse, my 40th birthday was approaching and all I could think was, wow, I'm a 40-year-old loser – jobless, man-less, and homeless. Great, let's celebrate.

I always thought that by 40, I would be who I was meant to be. There wouldn't be any need to start over. The first thing to go was my job. I had been on my job for 11 years and loved the place I'd made for myself there. I worked hard at excelling and was well liked and made really good money. I met so many amazing people there and made lifelong friends. I thought I would retire from this place one day. One thing my father taught me was to learn all I could so that I would always be an asset and employable. I've always done this, so I should be alright. I have a great resume and glowing references, so why am I still unemployed a year later?

Next was the house. Of course, this was a process. I always dreamed of purchasing my own home. I never wanted to go from my parents' house to my husband's house, and four years ago that dream became a reality. I was so excited, scared but excited to have my own home. It took my daughter a little while to warm up to the idea of not living with grandma and pop-pop, but her own room finally drew her in. We had a ball decorating and making the house our own. My dad and uncles put their landscaping, painting and carpentry skills to good use. I was honored to be able to host family gatherings traditionally held at Moms. I wanted to make my home as loving and welcoming as hers. And this home was full of family and laughter, but now it was over and all I have are memories. I'm grateful for the memories.

Last to go was the relationship. I had secretly loved him since I was 12 years old. Over the years, we became friends and built a bond. We understood each other then. We both went away to different colleges and embarked on our separate lives, still keeping in touch and talking often. It wasn't until we both moved back home that I had the nerve to tell him how I felt about him. We entered a relationship that I thought would last forever, ignoring all the signs that said it probably won't. It's funny how life experiences can change a person so much they are almost unrecognizable. The more time we spent together, it became evident that we were no longer in sync. Our paths were not experiencing any merges or even crossroads. I couldn't fathom how the man could be so very different from the boy. Why couldn't he be who I knew he could be or who I needed him to be? Maybe because this is who he's grown to be and not who I remembered. After much reflection, I came to the realization that he wasn't the only one who had changed. The woman was way different from the girl, and I wasn't the only one with cause to hesitate. Innately we were the same, but life had shifted our mindsets and added layers the other wasn't equipped or willing to handle. And so, the inevitable happened and we were no more. Quick and clean? Not so much. Lots of tears, hurt feelings and crushed expectations.

So, there I was. Forty, single, jobless and living in my old room at my parents. Feeling like a failure. I would stay up all night, get my daughter up, take her to school and come back, close the curtains (because I couldn't stand the light) and sleep until it was time to pick her up. This went on for weeks. I was exhausted and miserable and moving farther away from who I really was. I had worked so hard to obtain the status I had. I put my all into making a life and for it to disappear all at once and so fast was mind blowing. I was most definitely sitting on the side of the road in the breakdown lane. I didn't even have the strength to wave somebody down, but thanks be unto God for those He places in our lives who pay attention.

God? Wait, had I forgotten him? Of course not, I always pray. I grew up on prayer. My faith has always been an important part of my life, so how in the world had I gotten so far off course, so fast? And why do I feel so far from God now? My mom noticed my retreat and began to call me the same time every day for breakfast. I would decline until she wouldn't take no for an answer. She started her probe slowly because she never wanted to pry, but quickly moved into her motherly advice. *You need to shake this off and pull yourself together. You look a mess. My grandbaby needs you. So, you lost some things, you'll start over.* How Mom??? Where do I start? *You start at the beginning, in prayer.* Mom, I pray, I haven't stopped praying. *Yes, but are you listening?* Listening? Could I have been so busy talking that I wasn't listening for the answers?

My God encounters after this were very different from my previous. I was so busy complaining about what was going wrong in my life and begging God to fix it that I couldn't hear what He had to say. I couldn't even see that I was in the middle of a life shift. Yes, life as I knew it was ending, but it had to for me to become who I was really meant to be. I had greater in me but became complacent where I was. I had to start asking the questions, *God, what is it that you want from me? Where do I go from here? How do I get up from this place?*

The answers came in waves, but the process was not always easy. Starting over is hard work but worth it. I had to work twice as hard and be intentional about my every move. I put my newfound listening skills to work and followed instructions carefully. I didn't always agree with the path that was put before me, but I learned how to trust and obey. God knew better and saw further. The losses I suffered were preparing me for what was next. They forced me to reevaluate and change my mindset. His path set me in places that prepared me for business and cultivated me in ministry. These places and new people taught me real compassion and how not to be so judgmental. My perspective changed as did the trajectory of my life. I would have never chosen to be in ministry to the extent God was calling me to be. But, before I knew it, I had accepted my call to the pastorate of the church my father pastored for 20 years, I met and fell in love with the man that would become my awesome husband. I have forged my own career path, in business and authorship, and I no longer live with my parents. God even covered my credit by allowing my house to be a short sale instead of a foreclosure.

It was a hard road back, but I made it with God's help. He never left me alone through the process. He even put some very special people in my path to guide and push me toward my next steps. Once I opened my heart and ears and surrendered my will to His. He began to make the impossible, possible in my life and gave me the strength to breakthrough every barrier that I faced. In every life, breakdowns are inevitable, but breakthroughs are up to you.

❧

Jasmine L. Spencer

Dr. Jasmine L. Spencer is the Senior Pastor of *Resurrection Life Ministries Sounds of Praise Inc.*, in Bridgeport, CT. She is the host of *The Wholey Living* Podcast, broadcasting on iHeart, Podbean, Amazon Podcast, Spotify and Clubhouse.

Dr. Spencer is passionate about the ministry of restoration and strives to help others in any way possible. Pastor Spencer received a bachelor's degree in Biblical Studies and master's and doctorate degrees in Theology from His Excellence Theological Seminary.

Dr. Spencer has worked in the corporate and non-profit arena. She served on the Board of Directors of Building Broken Warriors. Dr. Spencer is a resident of Bridgeport, CT and is happily married to Apostle Robert L. Spencer. Together they have two beautiful and talented daughters, Ananda and Kiara Michele.

To connect with Dr. Spencer, follow her on FB @ Jasmine L. Spencer / Resurrection Life Ministries / Wholey Living Podcast, on Instagram @livingwholey20 and Clubhouse as Jasmine L Spencer.

Disintegrated Destinations
Doris Brown

*H*ave you ever purposely planned your desired destination and it fell apart? Have you ever received a prophecy of where you're going and what you'll be? Although it was spoken over your life it seemed to have crumbled before your eyes. Were you told that you make plans and have board meetings but fail in production? Have you ever felt like what you saw in the natural gave the impression that all of God's plans were gradually disintegrating? Let's define disintegrate: it is to break, to separate or lose intactness, breakup, deteriorate (worsen or decline), to become weaker or be destroyed by breaking, etc.

The intention of this spirit is to break a believer mentally, which causes unsound decisions. It will make every effort to assist the believer in losing their intactness or solid confidence in the God that they serve; to separate us from the genuine truth of what the Word of God clearly is. What is the Word of God? It is best described as infallible -

meaning incapable of making mistakes or being wrong, unerring, error-free, unfailing, faultless, and flawless. If this spirit can aid in leading you to sever your relationship with God because of a spoken word over you, it has succeeded. I encourage you to take down the culprit's devises that's been employed to demolish you. No longer accept declines or downhills, but break the back of the destroyer through the power of God.

I would like to draw your attention to something that I thought was amazing as a child, but at the same time I wasn't aware of the impending danger that it resembles. It was extraordinarily stunning to the individual that could see it, while at the same time creating conversations and stopping people in their tracks. The artwork of it had no assistance from man. It was a spider web, yes wait for it! The web was designed to attract insects and to inform the spider of any entangled insect fighting for its life. In a single day the entire web is replaced daily. The most important purpose of the spider web was to trap insects for food. For we know that the enemy is sly and cunning, he will attempt to entangle us by using things that aren't visible to the natural eye. The physical beauty of things can cause us to be lured into deception, and once we are trapped we suffer memory lapse of how to get out. If we can be distracted and ensnared by the captivating web that the enemy had spun, we will experience restricted momentum and be led to believe that the fight to acquire victory is no longer in us.

Well, time after time, I fell into alley ways of floor dropping pits that appeared to have held me for a lifetime, without an expiration date. Afterward the trenches seemed to be reality, so I became enveloped in mind-boggling thoughts of previous failure. I no longer had the confidence to fight my way out. Here I was, having a hot fudge sundae meltdown on a cold day feeling like all my dreams were shattered; while failing to realize that I was given an assignment and I was the driving force to put it into action. You see, this spirit of disintegrated destination never wanted me to acquire the God-given desired results. Our dependence on God's Word is crucial to fight against impending oppositions. The knowledge and obedience of the Word of God ushers us into extraordinary assurance to succeed. Therefore, recognizing that the power of a stable life should consist of the Word of God, fasting, praying and being submissively obedient.

As an infant I had something called a death rattle, which is a distinctive sound that a person makes as they are coming to the end of their life. There was an unpleasant sound signaling that I was near death. Not knowing that this death rattling was sent to destroy the destination of a child that was chosen by God to do great exploits. It was predicted that I would never come out of the whirl wind alive. You see, I was destined to die. My destination was being altered, well that was the plot and the plan. But, due to parents that know the power of prayer, every rattle sound and its purpose was summoned to leave my body and it rendered it powerless over my life.

We must deal with this spirit of disintegrated destinations that is in operation. This seed was aggressively implanted to rupture the God-given assignment. It also has the intentions to cause your missions to appear stillborn. It then moves to impair your beliefs to acquire total failure. The apparent cause is that someone introduced that seed to life. That same individual must neutralize the functionality of that spirit, meaning render it ineffective. Our actions and reactions are vital to this journey for we must not be ignorant concerning the opponents' devices. We must also be mentally and physically prepared to make use of our spiritual weapons.

The specific course mapped out involves testing in the areas of psychological and corporeal, to fortify the believer's stand against the wiles of the adversary. *Psychologically* meaning, the mental and emotional state of a person. *Corporeal* meaning, in the flesh or body of the person. Simply put: "arm yourself likewise" and know that we will be tested. With every desired choice of destination, the enemy's objective is to disintegrate and alter how you perceive it; to always be in opposition of the Word of God. When we grant the enemy access into our lives it opens the door to many portals. All entry doors must be shut. As we grow in Christ Jesus the Word of God must be our day-to-day bread to effectively combat the mission.

When all plans seem to be heading in a downward spiral, know that it's a sign to take your eyes off the situation. I want to encourage you through these scriptures, "I will lift up my eyes unto the hills, from whence cometh my help. My help cometh from the lord, which made heaven and earth," (Psalms 121:1-2). "Thou wilt keep in perfect peace, whose mind is stayed on thee: because he trusteth in thee," (Isaiah 26:3). Notice four things, (1) Place a spotlight on a higher place (the hills). (2) Divine help is accessible; keep your eyes fixated on your Help at all costs. (3) We can only have the perfect peace when we constantly keep our mind stayed on Jesus, (4) It is imperative that we persistently trust Him.

Now remain encouraged and consciously aware that your future destinations can be achieved by looking up to the hills as you position yourself above and beyond your circumstances.

Doris Brown

Apostle Doris Brown is the Founder and Senior Leader of Walk in Righteous Living Ministries in Waterbury CT. Her apostolic lifestyle demonstrates her love in rearing leaders to fulfill their God-given assignment. Apostle's love for souls is genuine, she endeavors to win and teach many for Christ so that God might be Glorified! Her aim is to consistently live victoriously in the presence of God as she steadfastly holds to the Word of the Lord.

Her motto is: But none of these things move me, neither count I my life dear unto myself, so that I might finish my course with joy, and the ministry, which I have received of the Lord Jesus, to testify the gospel of the grace of God. Acts 20:24

Love Mattered
Etta Hinton

*B*ut.... God? That was the question I embraced as I pondered with fear about the very core of my existence. Feelings of uncertainty crippled me at that moment, and I was unsure of my capabilities to do all that I thought I was called to do. I sat and cried from exhaustion because I didn't understand. I asked, "God, why is it almost impossible to do Your will, to please You, and to trust You?" The more I sat and thought, the deeper my thoughts were. My next set of questions sounded something like, "God, if You really called me, why are You making it so hard for me to do the things that You called me to do? Why is there a struggle with and for everything? Why is there a constant battle with everything? Why do my words get thrown back at me in defeat when I feel like I am obeying You?"

These were some of the most defining times in my ability to identify God even when I couldn't recognize Him. I had to make a conscious choice not to allow frustration to cripple me. I had to take the technique of fighting that I learned on this journey and apply it for this journey. I was insecure, battling for attention, wishing to be loved, lonely, depressed, and uncertain of who I was and wondering would I ever be anything.

One of the highlights of my life when I was younger was traveling back and forth to New York to see family and visit my old church. One day, I remember going down the highway on I-95 heading back home to Connecticut. We were coming from New York, and I was traveling with my loved ones. All of a sudden everything got quiet, my mind began to drift, and I suddenly felt myself slip into a dark place. It was a scary, cold, and dreary place. It was lonely and it felt eternal.

I remember feeling vulnerable and helpless and like my world was coming to an end. The tears rolled down my face and I began to breath deep and fast. I tried to hide it, but the pain screamed out before I could get control over it. My aunt reached back to me with a sweet and caring, yet stern voice and asked me questions that are now very vague, but one thing I do remember is she began to plead the Blood of Jesus over me and my mind. She told the devil that he could not have me, and he would not take my mind. I felt her powerful hands touch my head and my heart; it felt as if I was being electrocuted.

I remember her saying to me that I had to make a choice; that I needed to give God my life. I remember repeating "*the Blood of Jesus*" in my head, hoping it would do whatever my aunt believed that it would do. She turned back to her seat and we reached our destination. All I could remember was that I felt ashamed and hopeless.

I remember thinking to myself that the prayer didn't take! It didn't work! It will never work because it's me. God will never love me, God will never use me, God would never see me the way He sees and uses others. It was a moment that I will never forget, and even today it still brings on a sense of awakening and reminds me of my beginning. Back then, and sometimes today still, I make the mistake of comparing my accomplishments with others and scoring my life based off what others thought and said about me. The biggest mistake I ever made was not learning the voice of God and the characteristics of God for myself. Not knowing His real thoughts towards me caused me to live in fear, pain, doubt, despair, and disbelief.

From then on, my moments in church started to be ritualistic instead of purposeful. I remember going to church with an attitude. I had resentment in my heart, I didn't want anyone saying anything to me, and I just didn't want to be there! I thought everyone who spoke a word to me didn't like me because nothing was ever positive, and I thought that in order to make people leave me alone I had to be mean and unwelcoming. So, that was me – mean, unwelcoming, uncaring, and unbothered. Truth is, I was bothered.

I wanted to know: *why are all these people shouting and getting what I desire, but me?* What is so special about them? Why was I created to be a bad person that even God didn't want anything to do with me? God, what is wrong with me? I can recall even in the midst of all of these feelings I still felt a tug and a pull, and not only did I fight with the people, I also fought with God. I argued with Him and I said things like, "God, you want me to sing, but they're going to laugh at me. You want me to usher, but they keep calling me mean. You want me to teach Sunday school, but they won't come, especially because it is me." All I kept pondering on was the intense feeling of everything being a fight, and I am losing!

Then, something happened. I'm not sure what it was, but something caused me to give it (salvation) another try, and it worked! As I can recall, when I received the gift of the Holy Ghost, I was in a place of wanting God and all that He had for me. My faith was activated and I remember praising God and saying, "Lord, please give me the Holy Ghost." I remember saying, "I am not leaving without the Holy Ghost today." I let my Pastor know what I was expecting, and with my determination and my pastor's encouragement, I was now a new recipient of the gift. I mean, the way it happened, just like that; I asked, and He gave it to me. I was blown away.

Later on, I learned that I didn't have to beg for a gift, or work for it, but just asking was enough (Romans 10:9-10). But, although I now had the Holy Ghost, I also had to learn that if I never experience pain, hardship, and defeat, I would never know that with God comes "love, joy, peace, longsuffering, gentleness, goodness, faith, Meekness, and temperance" (Galatians 5:22-23).

From the car ride home from New York to this present moment I have served in many capacities and now I am the Senior Pastor of Restoration and Healing Ministries. Yes, the distraught teenager; the confused young lady; and the messy, angry, obnoxious, and hardheaded lady, went through challenging stages, but God was with me every step of the way and have proved to me that I am worth it and that I am and has always been loved.

❧

Etta Hinton

Pastor Etta Hinton was born to Sharon Grant and Arthur Bedford on January 6, 1976, in New York City, NY. Pastor Hinton spent her youth attending the Mount Pisgah Movement under the leadership of Bishop James Isaac Wilkins.

In 1994, Pastor Hinton made the brave decision to relocate to New Haven, CT with her then future husband, Minister Shannon Hinton. In 2007 she answered the call of Evangelist and in 2009 she was ordained as Elder. Pastor Hinton has also received her bachelor's degree in Psychology from the University of Phoenix, her first master's degree in Biblical Studies and Theology from Destiny Word of Faith College of Theology, a second master's degree in Human Services and an Addiction Counseling certificate as a post grad from Albertus Magnus College.

She is the Senior Pastor of Restoration and Healing Ministries and she has five beautiful children together with her husband.

From Unwanted to Loved Unconditionally

Alison Jaye

*W*ords may not be said directly to you, but words have power. Words once spoken, whether good or bad, have an effect and can affect the trajectory of a person's life. We have heard of generational curses, some would say generational cycles, which also covers generational labeling. Without knowing it, I was labeled a troublemaker, having no hope or a future, destined to end up like my mother – unmarried with a string of children, a Jezebel homewrecker. Words spoken over me before I was born, and for many years of my life. Before I knew the truth about my past, I was living with labels. Before I knew what labels were, they had been firmly stitched into the fabric of my life like in a piece of clothing, of who and what I would be. For many years I bought into them, I believed them, I lived them.

Born as the result of a violent encounter, my mother, nineteen-years-old and unmarried having only been in the country five years, was disbelieved by almost everyone. That's when it started: loose, a Jezebel, a baby-making machine by different men, and never amount to anything. The most bizarre was the prediction that she would have abortions every year. Someone went as far as writing that in a letter to my grandmother that lived in the USA. She was none of that, never had an abortion and only one child, but no one cared. The assumptions and accusations seemed to be more gratifying than the truth, the truth no one attempted to find out.

Like a self-fulfilling prophecy I acted out and rebelled. I dated men I had no business knowing, much less dating, and I got into bad company; giving the label makers the justification they needed to believe they were right about my mother and subsequently, me. I thought I didn't care, and acted like the words, those labels, didn't hurt. The reality was obvious to everyone but me; my lifestyle clearly showed I was hurting. I partied like a rock star. In the clubs from Thursday night to Monday night and at work every day. My friends were drug dealers and I got involved in relationships, situationships and entanglements that, looking back, I really shouldn't have been in. I was in abusive relationships with serial cheaters, was cheated on and, without knowing, cheated with.

On the outside, I had a great life, I was well-known, went to the best places, and met the right well-known people in the community, even a few celebrities. The reality: I was lonely and empty. My hobby was shopping, buying things I didn't need and things for people that only liked me for what they could get. I was broke, had a mountain of debt, and was looking for love in all the wrong places. I didn't think I could sink any further, until a trip to New York for a family wedding. I was almost 30 years old when an aunt decided, out of the blue, to ask, "Have you ever wondered who your father is?" Not knowing where the conversation was heading, I answered, "Well, yeah, sometimes." I wasn't prepared or expected what came next. She told me that my mother, "said" she was assaulted, by someone well-known to our family. I could hear by the emphasis on "said" she didn't believe my mother. She went into detail, telling me everyone in the family knew. She talked and talked, I drifted between hearing her and my thoughts.

I'm not sure which emotion I felt first or the strongest, shame or anger. It explained so much about why the relationship with my mother had been so strained, and at times, almost non-existent. I thought she hated me and didn't want me. All those years of hurt and pain with no outlet, compounded by being talked about and unfairly negatively labeled. The first thing I did when I arrived back to London was called my mother and ask her if it was true. She confirmed it was; she told me exactly what had happened. I learned the motives behind why my aunt had told me: she was one of the label makers. I was sitting in the middle of my living room floor in a daze. It was true and everyone knew. Why had no one, especially my mother, ever told me?

I reached for the bottle of 500 pain pills and took them. Between tears with each handful, everything that had been going wrong with my life came to mind. The empty meaningless relationships, the debt, the relationship with my mother, everything came flooding over me like an emotional tsunami. I wanted it to end, to be over. I hoped I would go to sleep and that would be the end of the pain. After a few minutes, I felt excruciating stomach cramps and began vomiting. I thought it was blood; turns out it was the red dye in the tablets. Terrified, I called an ambulance, and they took me to the hospital to flush out all of the pills.

Because of the strength of the pills and the amount I had taken, they were convinced I would suffer with liver disease for the rest of my life. They ran tests but the doctors were amazed. Miraculously, there was no liver damage. Hours later, I left the hospital. It hit me, I had been given another chance, a chance to get my life together, to break free from all the labels I had been given and that I gave myself. The most important thing I needed to do was go to my mother. We needed healing. I didn't know where or how to start; I just knew it needed to be done. Sometimes we miss opportunities out of fear and uncertainty. The truth is we don't have to have it all planned and mapped out, we just need the courage to take that step.

We agreed, we needed to fix us. We needed healing emotionally, mentally and spiritually, to forgive ourselves and those who hurt and labeled us. I realized I was holding on to the labels, like a security blanket. They were familiar, they were my identity. I learned to live in dysfunction.

I'm not going to say it was easy, or that magically we were in a good place. It took months of talking, praying, crying, and some heated conversations. It meant being intentional and sticking with it, not being afraid to have hard conversations, being transparent, and vulnerable. If you are prepared to do the work and stay the course, the results are worth it. Now, my mother is my best friend, the person I go to for advice. We have a beautiful relationship. People struggle to believe it was once at a point where we barely spoke to each other.

We were given a second chance and determined to not waste it. We are free; free from being defined by negative labels; free from believing the negative perceptions. We can all live with that freedom. We must believe that we deserve it, because the truth is, we all do. "What the enemy meant for evil, God turned it for our good."

❧

Alison Jaye

Alison Jaye is the author of the Ethel Mae books, a qualified Certified Life Coach, Stress Management Therapist, an Ordained Minister, Public Speaker and Podcaster, born and raised in London, England.

Having experienced many challenges in her life, she was able to reach and help young people overcome many of the obstacles and challenges they face. Many had been through traumatic life changing experiences, in need of guidance and help to push past where they had been and on the road to a better life ahead. Her coaching grew to include men and women.

Alison believes we all have it within to live the best abundant life possible that God has promised. She has made it her aim to help as many as possible realize their potential. Her coaching style is a little different, she believes, in order to move forward, you have to unpack the baggage of the past.

When Life Forces You to Eat Lemons
Vette Green

The Sour Taste

They don't tell you that your world will be rocked. They don't tell you that life as you know it will be shaken up. They don't let you in on the big SECRET about change. A lot has to and will come with it. Who I thought I was is not who I am, not for real for real, as the kids say. I hit my rock bottom, looked around and realized it was very painful but my pain didn't come from the impact, though I felt it. The impact came and went, leaving a big hole in my life and yet I continued to try and dig my hole deeper.

My pain came from my own self sabotage and complacency. I was okay being mediocre and not exerting too much pressure on my own neck. I was okay being a part of the walking dead club. In this club I didn't have to do much work, I could just be. I didn't have to shower, I didn't have to comb my hair, and I could wallow in misery and not be looked at as different. I didn't have to work, but if I did

I was required to push myself to outgrow my position and search for better. I could just be. But God had a different plan for me and if you are reading this he does for you too.

Yes, I hit my rock bottom, but the light inside of me still held a flicker of life. My soul refused to die and so my whole world was shaken when I finally gave myself permission to stand back up and stop eating the dirt that was thrown on top of me. My whole world had to be shaken to rustle up the part of me that wanted to die and to rustle up the dry bones that had become accustomed to barely getting by and being okay with it. I felt alone and more often than not, as if nobody could understand me so when the going got rough I decided to check out.

I started numbing that pain that keeps us up at night tossing and turning. Drinking, drugs, and after a while, self-loathing, and disrespect to my very being became a huge part of my daily routine. I would wake up, pop some pain pills and Xanax to get through my day. By noon I had to pop some more because if I woke up I did not want to be involved with life. I wanted to just walk around and be left alone or swim off in the depth of nothingness until night time came and I could add Ambien to my mix along with vodka and hope that death would come and take over… BUT GOD!

The Mixing

It's the baby steps for me. The baby steps when you add them all up equate to a lot of growth. Those baby steps are what lead us to our next destination. I had to take baby steps to lead me right here: co-authoring a book. Even now as I write this I'm amazed at how fast God works when you are willing to work too. I give it all to Him and I'm not religious by any means. I love my Creator and I understand that I come from something great. A name has been placed on them and for me it's God. God has gotten me through some tough times and most of the time I didn't have to ask, He just did it.

That Presence knew who I was before I began to walk down this road of self-discovery. That Presence knew who I was when my biological dad wrapped his hands around my mother's throat and almost took hers and my life while she was six months pregnant with me. That Presence also knew who I was when at 18, I was hospitalized with a blood clot the size of a grapefruit inside my lung. The doctors were amazed that I was still alive and told me my lung had not even grown to an adult size because of this blood clot. So, when you hear me say BUT GOD, you may be able to understand why I give Him my praise and glory.

New Year, New Me

There are givers and takers in this world and it's a must that you find out just what you are dealing with when you allow certain energy into your life. Not everyone who enters your life is there to stay, I've learned. I have had some that entered to be lessons only and meant to rekindle a flame in me that had died out. They came across my path to give me that *oomph* I needed to get back up and move on. You may have encountered a person that came into your life and sparked those flames that had dwindled from a prior broken heart; I know I did. He inflated my heart and body as if I were one of those blow up toys you win at an amusement park. I felt like he breathed life into my soul and flesh and brought the dead inside of me back to life. But, unfortunately my resuscitator wasn't strong enough to handle the shine of my light, so he couldn't stay; it wasn't meant to be forever anyhow. I just didn't know that at the time. My heart and body thought it was but my mind (when I allowed it to override my emotions) knew it wasn't meant to be.

I tried to hold on because my resuscitator helped me realize that I am sexy, my resuscitator made me feel beautiful and sensual, young and capable of being loved again. You see, less than six months prior to meeting him I tried to take myself out of this world for the third time. The saying is three strikes, and you are out, but this was a three strikes and I was in a better place to become a higher, more elevated version of who I am supposed to be all along.

The Sweetness

In closing, as I turn the pages through each chapter of my life, and I sit and "unpack" I realize I had to go through things in order to grow to become Vette Green. Tests and lessons that I passed and failed in order to mold me into the person God promised I could be. Some of those lessons had me in tears praying to GOD to take the hurt away. There were also lessons that had me angry with God questioning why I was going through some of these obstacles when other people I knew who I felt deserved that type of treatment seemingly were living their best life, or the best lie I now see.

Everything I am learning has led me to realize that God

will help mold and shape you into who you are meant to be. When I became open to receiving the information and insight that was being provided to me about my life it was like an "aha" moment. Some people, places and things that go in and out of your life may be brief moments, not forever. The experiences are meant to be held onto and used as tools, not weapons against ourselves which many of us fall prey to – in other words, the self-sabotage. Those who were meant to be in your life will remain and those who aren't will fade away. The moral of my story is no matter what happens, no matter how difficult it may seem, keep going. The other side of that "thing" is where you will find your strong side waiting.

※

Vette Green

Vette Green is a Transformational Coach out of Chicago, IL. Raised in a small town outside of Buffalo, NY. She is currently working on her first manuscript.

Questioning the Past
"If God does not value me...who will?
Erika Erkard

For years I denied the fact that childhood sexual abuse marred my psyche to the point that I was emotionally numb. And on the rare occasions that I did feel something (hurt, disappointment, loneliness), I compartmentalized those emotions; secreting them away from prying eyes. The severity of the abuse I endured affected the way I perceived myself and the way I envisioned God would respond to me. I desperately wanted to know God as Father, but I was so ashamed of that desire I kept it buried deep within myself. It simply made no sense to me that I should trust a Sovereign God who would not protect a child from the sadistic appetites of a pedophile. Why would God want a daughter who wasn't worth protecting and whose pain cried out constantly from a gaping wound of shame?

My breakdown occurred at six years old and I've spent a lifetime fighting for my breakthrough. Tormented by a myriad of insecurities, grasping God's unconditional love proved nearly impossible for me. Years of systematic, unfettered physical abuse, administered to make me pliable, fearful and accommodating broke my spirit and obliterated my self-esteem. I was limited in the ability to trust God's love for me. It has literally taken a lifetime for me to confront my pain and ask God the hard questions that I hoped might bring some clarity to my existence. The most challenging question I posed to myself was interwoven in my desire to know, but inability to accept God as my father. How could a loving father abandon his own child...yet claim to love her? How could God sit silent for so long and not move to defend me? Repeatedly these questions were posed to God in my mind, as hot and bitter tears streamed down my face, watering the ground of insecurity and anger in my heart.

How is it that no responsible adult in my life ever fought for me? Who decided my existence was inconsequential? What criteria did they use to arrive at their conclusion to ignore my suffering? Who did they consult with? Did anyone consider how their final synopsis of who I was or wasn't might affect my future? Did they consider the fact that I might be emotionally damaged forever by the deliberate and systematic abuse being leveraged at my head (my intellect) and my heart (my emotions)? Whose idea was it to reduce my self-esteem to zero, obliterating my sense of self-worth, reducing me incident by incident, shame by shame, defilement by defilement? Whose idea was it to belittle, demean, and degrade me to the point that my childhood fantasies were fashioned around cloaks of invisibility and hidden places, rather than fairy princess dresses, crowns and handsome knights in shining armor? Who decided that before a young man even made me blush for the first time, I would look past what he represented in terms of youthful innocence, into a woman's experienced knowing of lustful flesh?

What happened to the child I should have been?

Where are her bows and ribbons? Where are her poufy pink dresses and white patent leather shoes with baby doll socks for Sunday morning dress up? Who took her pastel colored barrettes and replaced them with the knowledge of things she should have never been made aware of? Who, who, who did this to the precious baby that should have been me? Who was it that shut off the gleam of naivete in her eyes, to be replaced with emboldened stares? Who taught her to speak with her eyes? Why does she do that at such a young age? Who taught her to hide and lie and keep secrets and look away like a stranger from faces she knows all too well? The faces of her abusers are familiar to her and she is familiar to them; they know each other well. Where is this little girl's innocence? Who has it? I demand to know who will restore it! Can anyone? Who will wash her self-esteem, shine it up, and give it back to her in a brand new box (body), smelling like jasmine soap and baby lotion?

Why didn't someone have enough compassion to rescue her? Who ignored her dilemma and ripped her virginal blindfold off just as she was blossoming into everything that precious little girls should be? Who stole her giggle? Why doesn't she sing to her stuffed animals? Does she have any? Does anyone think it strange that she doesn't touch dolls, or play with toys? Does she have friends to laugh and skip in the sunshine with? Why not? Why is she ashamed to express herself freely? Why doesn't she play games with the other children? Why do they shy away from her? Do they know she is not pure like they are? Why is she self-conscious, covering herself, hiding her form under shapeless clothing, not wanting to show her body, yet enslaved by it? She is in prison; her jailer is her sexuality. Who put her there? Where is the key that unlocks her healing and wholeness? Who was so cruel to show her the grotesque underbelly of real life before her eyes had time to adjust to the murky shadows of fleeting dreams that would never materialize for her?

There was a time in my life when I was tormented by these questions and the lack of answers I received. I thought the answers would give me closure, but after years of frustration I began to realize that more than anything, I needed the peace of God. So, I let the questions go and began to pray earnestly for healing that would release peace and spiritual breakthrough to my spirit. Our God is so faithful, showering me with His unconditional love each day, simply because I am His child.

Psalm 5:11-12, "But let all those that put their trust in thee rejoice: let them ever shout for joy, because thou defendest them: let them also that love thy name be joyful in thee. For thou, Lord wilt bless the righteous; with favour wilt thou compass him as with a shield.

❧

Erika Erkard

Though she was born in Florida, Erika Erkard has been a resident of New Haven, Connecticut "The Elm City", for most of her life. Due to her family's periodic and often sudden relocations, she attended three different middle schools and three separate high schools, which exposed her to many of the complex and ever evolving dilemmas facing families in transition. Raised primarily by a single mother with severely limited resources and support, she became acquainted at an early age with the uniquely distressing pressures single parent homes are often subjected to. Although her childhood was riddled with varied forms of abuse, neglect, and abandonment; in the midst of those life challenges she developed an intense desire to persevere, succeed and empower others.

Married for 16 years to Thomas Erkard, Jr., she is thankful to God for her husband's unfailing love, support, and encouragement. Her professional career in management for a highly successful architectural lighting company spanned 20 years and she is currently embarking on a second career as an independent entrepreneur. Erika is a writer and published author, holding a Bachelor of Theology degree from the Christian Leadership Bible College. She is the host of "Strength for The Journey", a weekly empowerment broadcast and facilitates an online mentorship resource group "Treasures in Earthen Vessels", which is designed to support and encourage women through the mentorship process. Erika is a lover of God and actively seeks out opportunities to assist, bless, and strengthen the Body of

Christ at large. One of her favorite scriptures is Philippians 4:13, "I can do all things through Christ which strengtheneth me"; and her favorite quote is *"Every day I am becoming what I shall be!"*

Bananas: Victory over Rejection
Shanika Wagner

They say you're only as sick as your secrets. I should know firsthand; I've not only harbored secrets, but I've been the secret. Yes, rejection was the story of my life until I decided to take that power back. I had to learn that I was good enough, wanted and loved. I'm sharing my story to help someone else who feels like they will never overcome or see themselves on the other side of rejection.

This journey isn't easy. It doesn't feel good when you open those wounds that you've bandaged for so long. You must first admit that there is a wound. Then you consistently clean, treat, and cover... until you take off the bandage one final time and no longer require it. So, it is with our hearts and minds. Hallelujah!

HOW IT WENT...

I was always timid as a child. No one saw the broken little girl who never felt like she fit in. I never felt good enough. I was continuously bullied and told I was ugly, stupid, and fat-shamed constantly before I could even spell self-esteem. I was chosen last and learned to put myself last as a result. I was very tender-hearted, compassionate, shy, and empathetic as a child. I still am as an adult. I just had to get back to the little girl buried beneath a crumbled innocence and so many pieces of a broken heart. I had to find her to heal her so that the essence of who I genuinely am could shine through and permeate my entire existence.

As a child, I was indirectly taught that my feelings and opinion didn't matter. For years I believed this because within several relationships it was said to me. Being labeled a drama queen, crazy, and too sensitive caused me to devalue my feelings and thoughts. This was almost the death of me several times. Whenever I felt dismissed and unwanted, I shifted to a lonely place. Even in a crowd of people, happy and smiling, I was screaming, "CAN ANYONE SEE ME?!" The danger, for me, was the combination of my sensitivity, being bullied, and being disrespected, which lead to suicidal thoughts that eventually lead to attempts.

It had gotten so bad during my teenage years that I would have anxiety attacks and would break down and cry before leaving the house for school in the morning. No one in my family had ever gone to a therapist or counselor, so I didn't even know what help I needed. I suffered alone in a house full of people. Then there was food. Food was my friend. While most girls were trying to look cute, I felt ugly and was told I was funny looking, so I figured, "Why bother?" Of course, looking back now, I was beautiful. I just couldn't see it because I rarely heard it.

I learned to live with or to be a secret since childhood. I can remember a conversation my dad had with my birth mom that affected the way I thought of myself and further fed the rejection within me. He had no idea I heard the conversation because I was supposed to be asleep.

During high school and entering young adulthood, guys would always express their "feelings" for me in private. Mostly because I was the fat girl and an embarrassment. Most of the time, there was always someone spewing sexually charged venom and disrespect. I slowly began to internalize the idea that it was what I deserved. I entered several relationships with men who were, quite frankly, unavailable to me. They were either unavailable mentally, emotional, or simply unavailable.

I got in these relationships because they appealed to my brokenness and made me feel wanted. They also appealed to the part of me that had commitment issues. I was using these relationships as band aids. Unfortunately, I needed more bandages as they came to an end. I became an alcoholic and promiscuous. These behaviors were completely uncharacteristic of who I was.

HOW IT'S GOING...

I'm learning to not allow my trauma to speak for me. I left those relationships and began to believe that I was more and that I deserved more. I also take advantage of therapy. As Paul said, "I count not myself to have apprehended: but this one thing I do, forgetting those things which are behind, and reaching forth unto those things which are before, I press." (Philippians 3:13-14). As I go, there is more to unpack; the walls that were built weren't built overnight. Even if they all came crashing down at once, there would be so much debris and residue to work through just to reveal the foundation of who I am.

Yes, we create a new foundation through Christ and deliverance unlocks the door and frees you from a prison, but what happens next? I had to go back to that little girl and admit what happened to me. I then had to seek help and work through it.

Think of bananas. Sometimes they get bruised badly, or they sit a little while after ripening. They may still be good fruit that we can eat, yet we've conditioned ourselves to view the whole thing as damaged, no good, or TRASH! We think, *"Just throw them out."* However, those same overripe bananas can be used and transformed with just a few additions to make amazing things. Things like banana bread, ice cream, muffins, etc. We think they are no good because the color has changed, the fruit flies have started to gather, and the texture is softer. It is, however, quite the contrary.

They are imperfect, yet in perfect condition to be made new! Now that they have been softened, they are ready to be wholly transformed, and the essence is being released so strong that it won't lose its flavor during the transformation process. HALLELUJAH! See yourself as that bruised banana. You've been rejected because there are some bruises and imperfections. People have gathered waiting on you to die. Some have even thrown you away. I want you to know that now is the perfect time to allow God to transform you completely. He wants to do a new work, according to Isaiah 43:19.

What He adds will make you sweeter and change your identity. Most of all, it will keep you from dying before you see the good things God has prepared for you. You are NOT trash,; not destroyed. GOD STILL WANTS YOU! Never forget that. You can be transformed if you yield and allow God to heal you. As a six-time college dropout who will be completing my first degree with honors, a shy kid who has now released two singles, will be featured in an upcoming movie, and owns a t-shirt boutique, I can tell you, God has more for you!

I had to take back my power and speak over myself every day. If nothing else, repeat this to yourself until your behavior displays the belief thereof and you see the manifestation in your life: *"I am loved. I am cared for. I am thought of. I am healed. God has me on His mind. I am chosen. I am capable."*

Shanika Wagner

"LET THE HIGH PRAISES OF GOD BE HEARD!" That's the motto of gospel singer-songwriter and entrepreneur, Shanika Wagner.

Born into a family where music and singing bring joy amid sorrow, Shanika began singing at the tender age of 2 years old. Then, certain traumatic events took place, causing her to become a timid and introverted child. As a result, Shanika wouldn't sing in public and she suffered with social anxiety until the age of 17 after she had given her life to Christ.

Once in the care of Christ, her confidence began to build, not in skill, but the anointing of God. Shanika is a licensed and ordained Elder under her current Pastor, Apostle Bryan Andrew Wilson and church Freedom of Atlanta.

Musically, she has written for and recorded with the National Capital Baptist Convention Choir for their first project, "Reaching the World for Jesus." She is a well-known participant in the National I.R.O.C.K. choir and singing group 3Fold Praise. She released her debut single titled, *All Hail the King*, in September 2018 and follow-up single, *Cornerstone* on September 9, 2020.

Shanika is also an actress and a phenomenal cook. She operates an online t-shirt boutique, Lady Neek's Treasures, and food delivery service, Auntie Nika's Soul Food. She has a heart for worship as well as a call to share healing, strength and encouragement to other women through Lady Neek Ministries. Happily serving others, Shanika collaborates with local churches and organizations in the neighboring city of Washington, D.C. She has, on occasion, prepared and served food for the House of Ruth Women's Shelter in Washington, D.C.. She is a constant participant in food distribution with the St. Teresa's of Avila Parish in Washington, D.C. Her first love is children and she often run social media fundraisers for "No Kid Hungry."

She believes in faith activation through kingdom works (James 2:14). Her constant prayer is that God's presence would overtake her so that lives would be changed as she gives him the Glory through worship and service to others.

The Reset
Margo Bullock

When we were initially introduced, he was simply a business partner. We would hang out making money together, building a friendship. People couldn't seem to get enough of him. Wherever we went he was the life of the party. I didn't view him as others did, but after months of witnessing the attention given to him, my curiosity got the best of me. I decided to explore my options with him. The partnership bloomed into a full blown relationship, which I kept a secret. Only those in our circle knew that I had decided to commit to him.

After a year, the relationship started to take a turn for the worse. He had become possessive and controlling; demanding all of my time. He had successfully lured me away from my family, and I no longer spent time with my friends. My time became consumed with him, his friends, and whatever they wanted to do. The relationship became harder to hide because it was apparent that I had lost my way. It was now public knowledge to my family and friends that I completely depended on him. My entire mindset and makeup had changed.

Others would often question our courtship, wondering why I would ever get involved with him. I'd be met with comments such as, *"He's no good for you,"* or *"He's going to ruin your life…if he doesn't kill you first."* When I would hear them, I would silently agree, but I couldn't rationalize the bond we shared, so it was like noise in my ears. Most people labeled and belittled me because I refused to give up my relationship. Some had offered to help get me away from him, but I wasn't strong enough to walk away at the times the offers were presented. It wasn't until year two that I really wanted out of the toxic relationship.

I started having attacks in my chest, as if I were having a heart attack. I rushed to the emergency room, and they couldn't find anything wrong, though they did advise the valves in my heart were clogged. I didn't bother to ask how that could happen because I knew it was due to the stress of still being with him. Silently, I began to come to terms that I needed out of this unhealthy relationship that had me bound. One Sunday morning, as I was watching a church service on TV, my chest started to hurt. My family had gone to church so I was home alone. The church had a number at the bottom of the screen for prayer requests. I called, but didn't get an answer. It was at that moment that a sense of urgency arose in me — I knew that I had to be set free. I felt an urgency in me and called the 700 Club for prayer; a woman answered the phone and asked how she could help. I explained my situation and she quickly gave me instructions to follow. I fell on my knees in my room, and she began to pray for me. My entire being was in agreeance with her prayer and from that moment, I was set free.

When I got up from the prayer, I felt the heavy weight of the soul tie removed from me. I had been released from his stronghold. I was so grateful to GOD for never turning his back on me and him keeping his agreement to heal, deliver, and set me free. I knew my grace and mercy was running out and only GOD could save me. There may be a question of who caused me all of this grief and pain — Crack Cocaine was his name. People debate GOD'S existence, but I'm a witness that he is alive and he's a promise keeper. He tells us that he will never leave nor forsake us, and he never does. I believed with my heart that he would deliver me and he did.

My journey ended in 1994 and I've spent time seeking wisdom and knowledge from GOD regarding that era of my life and the purpose. It has been made clear that I'm one of the chosen vessels for this assignment. It is written, "No temptation has overtaken you except such as is common to man; but GOD is faithful, who will not allow you to be tempted beyond what you are able, but with the temptation will also make the way of escape, that you may be able to bear it." (1 Cor. 10:13) The journey wasn't just for me, it was a part of my discipleship to help others be set free. It's amazing that during that time GOD was working his plan through me.

God's ways are not our ways, so what He doesn't always make sense to us. God will get the GLORY out of our lives; there is no way to rationalize his power. Our job is to give him glory. If your soul is tied and in bondage to an addiction, no matter what it may be, I encourage you to cry out to GOD and allow him to heal you. There are times in our lives when the burdens of life's circumstances are so heavy that we don't have the strength to pray for ourselves. Don't let that stop you from seeking the healing and deliverance you need.

There will always be a voice (Satan) trying to convince you that nobody can help you and nobody loves you. The best time to make the call is when you hear that voice trying to convince you, because we know that the devil is the father of lies. His job is to destroy us and keep us under his wings. He knows he has been defeated for eternity and wants to destroy as many souls as he can. Once we allow GOD to heal us, Satan knows that we can tear his kingdom down. He knows who we are in the kingdom of God; his goal is to prevent us from knowing our true identity. He is in the business of stealing our identity and rewriting GOD'S original plan for our lives. We have given him enough of our time, talents, and souls. It's time to cancel our contracts with the devourer and connect with the restorer of our souls. Let's continue to cast our cares on the only one that loves us enough to forgive us and reset our lives, giving us another chance to get it right. The scripture below is evidence that GOD will hear you and work a miracle through you:

> *"I cried to HIM with my mouth, And He was extolled with my tongue. If I regard iniquity in my heart, The Lord will not hear. But certainly God has heard me; He has attended to the voice of my prayer. Blessed be God, who has not turned away my prayer, Nor His mercy from me."* (Psalms 66:17-20)

Margo Bullock

Margo Bullock is the founder and CEO of Ready for Change Inc., a foundation that focuses on a holistic approach of improving the quality of one's life. Through Margo's experiences, she has discovered a passion for guiding those who suffer from any type of addiction to freedom. Her passion, coupled with her faith in GOD, help keep her vision alive. Among the many hats she wears, she is an independent travel agent, licensed insurance broker, and an aspiring author. In her free time, she can be found enjoying a live play, traveling, swimming, or bowling.

Fire Formed

Dana Williams-Taylor

hey told me I was fearfully and wonderfully made. Well, God certainly made a miracle out of me. Look at me, a 16-year-old black girl, pregnant, and dating the star of the football team. Everybody wants a piece of me, from boys to men, and even women too. Since I was six years old, they molested me and made me suffer in silence. "Don't tell nobody!" they said to me. "This is our little secret. Besides, nobody's going to believe a kid." They couldn't wait to get their hands on me. Every night when I bathed, a voice would tell me to go to the mirror and pull my hair out. It would tell me to do what it said, or it would kill my brothers and sisters. It called my brothers and sisters out by name and said it would kill them all! I didn't want them to be hurt, even though nobody wanted to play with me. I was the weird one. I was the slow one, the retarded one. I loved them, but back then nobody loved me. That's why I found somebody who did love me.

That's where I was mentally, in 1986. I later married the

boy from high school, but I found out he didn't know what love was either. He ended his football pursuit, turned down scholarships, and decided to stay with me and the baby. But he became angry and abusive. We divorced after years of torment and four children. I remember feeling scared, sad, and ashamed; I felt like I didn't want to live. I remember being hospitalized because my husband had beaten me so bad my face was disfigured. The walls of my home had been painted with blood. My children's screams echoed down the halls and our tears rinsed the floors. We ran to shelters in efforts to escape him, but he always found a way to get us. All my life I had been seeking refuge in the wrong things, but as I said, God was making a miracle out of me.

The world would see me as a statistic. I was another contribution to the sexual abuse victim rates, the divorce rates, the domestic violence rates, the poverty rates, the teen pregnancy rates, and the depression rates. It didn't help that I was from a Christian family. I was a statistic and a tool for the devil to use against the proclamation of the gospel, or so I thought.

The voice I heard for years as a child ceased when one night. I heard the voice and the voice told me to pull out my hair. I will never forget my mom was in the kitchen talking on the phone, praying and counseling someone. And this certain night I was tired, and I didn't want to listen to the voice and the voice told me to pull out a big amount of my hair. I didn't want to, so I said, "No more I've had enough!" The voice said, "Do it now!" I began to cry because I pulled a big chunk of hair and I started to scream, and my mother heard me screaming and crying. I heard Mom tell the person on the phone that she had to go because her child is in trouble.

I heard the voice saying don't tell or you will die, and he started to call all of my siblings' names. Mom said to me, "Dana…You can tell me." I began to cry and shake my head. "No, I can't." My mom said, "Oh yes you can!" I told her that if I told her what was wrong they were going to kill her and all my brothers and sisters and daddy too. My mom said "No" as if she saw the person in me and I told her what the voice told me. My mom said, "The blood of Jesus is against you! You have no rights in Dana! Get out in the name of Jesus!" Momma prayed until I could not hear the voice and when it was time for me to take a bath, I didn't hear that voice ever again.

Despite the statistics and labels people put on me God showed me the greatest label I would have been called: His daughter. Today I have a wonderful life that is a complete 180 from where I was in my youth. I know how to fight for myself in the spirit and I have used the things the devil meant to kill as empowerment for people all over the world. Through this deliverance I have found my life to be better than ever, and the best is yet to come. I have rooted my hope in Jesus and, by pursuing purpose, I am walking into abundant living.

We know the skin may be cut, scab, and heal; it does not do so without a scar. The same is true for me. I did not go through all the turmoil and come out without a scar. What's powerful is that scar serves only as a reminder of God's grace in my life. I say this candidly admitting I made many mistakes along the way. I made decisions that were not in my best interest, and I didn't always act in the best manner. Yes, I wanted to quit. Yes, I not only believed the labels put on me, but I placed false labels on myself. Yes, I was flat out broken. Yes, I hurt people too. This is why I love God so much. He doesn't base His love on my flaws and faults. He doesn't bless me because I earned it, He blesses me because He loves me and calls me his own. That same God loves you too.

You may have been fooled, but you are not a fool! You may have been thrown out and dismissed, but you are not trash! You may have been told you are nothing, but to the right person, you are everything! You matter! You are powerful! You are amazing! And now is the time to show the whole world who you truly are! Don't know how? Thankfully, God has led me to become an empowerment strategist and I aim to help people like you not only redefine themselves, but take practical steps towards developing that life they deserve! I thought God had left me, but my mother spent years covering us in prayer and she taught me what it meant to trust God even through your suffering. Because she instilled values in me when I was young, today I choose to be powerful, not petty. I choose to not be a victim and be victorious. All of life is a choice! Even when it doesn't feel that way. The good news is you don't have to walk through these choices alone. So, be encouraged! Trust God! Take actions that will change your life forever as you transform into the greatest version of yourself you have ever seen. Greatness is in you. By the way, I love you, and there is nothing you can do about it!

Author's Note

I am Dana Williams Taylor, founder of Be Nice, a company birthed in random acts of kindness and sharing the grace God has shown me. You can find me on Facebook at 2daybenice (business page). We stream live broadcasts every Tuesday, for *"Tell the Truth Tuesday"*, and Friday, for *"Freedom Friday"*, at 5pm Central Standard Time on each day. I thank you for taking the time to read my story and it is my prayer that you are encouraged to push on and let your light shine in dark places. I hope to see you soon!

❧

Dana Williams Taylor

Who is this innovative powerhouse that just seems to have appeared out of nowhere? Well, Dana Taylor is one of the most God fearing and inspirational women you will ever meet. She totes the "Be Nice" brand, which is an entity built on showing kindness in a world that glorifies violence, showing love in a world that finds reason to hate, and bringing joy to your life when it seems that everyone is at war.

Dana knows the power of prayer, taught to her by her parents who pastored a small church in Milwaukee, WI, Dana's hometown. Her parents introduced her to Christ at a young age and instilled values of love and forgiveness. These values became a monumental part of her life as she went on to experience molestation in her youth. The world she anticipated was more of a utopia than a reality. As the sixth child of children in the household, Dana expected to be able to rest in safety and encounter the love she was taught to give. Instead, she collided with jealousy, envy, hatred, greed, selfishness, pain, suffering, and rejection.

Dana is a survivor! From experiencing molestation from age six to 13, from men and women, to being beaten and raped during her first marriage, Dana never gave up. She has five children who have grown up and begun families of their own. The love she was taught, she instilled in them. She has been diligent in empowering them to be their best. Dana believes it's not how you start, it's how you finish. She grew up believing she was stupid, believing she had no value and even became suicidal. But today, she is an empowerment coach, married to a man who loves and supports her. Freed from shame and condemnation, she knows her worth and is an empowerment strategist with an edge. That edge is the Lord Jesus Christ.

Dana helps people take ownership of their lives and remove negative thoughts, behaviors, and habits. She teaches the power of mindfulness and affirmations. God has given us all we need to live life with power and freedom to act and think without restraint or hindrance. She has developed a four-step "make it happen plan" to help you build the life you deserve.

Blindness Led to the Vision
Shalonda Chaney-White

could hardly wait to turn sixteen and enter early adulthood. My peers were all dating, and although I had a few boyfriends through my freshman year of high school, it was nothing serious. I always desired to have a known relationship where everyone knew who I was dating. Although that was my fantasy, it didn't quite happen that way. Instead of letting nature play its part I wanted to rush the process, and we all know by now when you don't give it time you may end up with someone you'll regret. I finally met someone through my cousin; we actually went to school together. I never found him attractive but after spending time with him he was cool and I was ready to start this new relationship. Little did I know I would never be ready for what was coming in my future.

Our time together turned out to be the longest five years of my life. I met 10 different guys in one body; I find out who I was dealing with as the days changed. I soon found out that his main character was a deranged abuser. I am a domestic violence survivor who encountered trauma, anxiety, and depression. Today, I am living with a disability. I am blind in my left eye, but you may not notice unless you notice the physical changes, such as the grayness in my eye from the lack of oxygen and the deterioration process.

A year into this relationship we knew we wanted to be together. We started planning when we were going to move, and although my family didn't like him I was determined to live my life the way I wanted to. I lived with my mother and grandmother, and no matter how much I got caught up with this guy I could not be stopped because I thought I was grown; so grown that I was lying about my whereabouts and spending weekends alone with him.

The first altercation caught me off guard; we were at our favorite low-key hotel. On this Sunday I was dressing to go home when I felt him attack me. I only knew that I needed to fight back, but why? As the tussle drew to an end, I found out it was because my body shape was showing through my clothes. This was the beginning, and clearly not the end, of the abuse. As months progressed in the relationship so did his insecurities. I was randomly accused of cheating. Every time we went out, he'd say some guy was looking at me or vice versa; which was a delusion he created and believed. He enjoyed the false accusations; it was actually building up his masculine ego. Once we'd leave the premises, he satisfied it with a physical attack.

As I approached my 18th birthday, we decided to move. My grandmother gave us furniture, dishes, and allowed me to take my bed. We moved in an apartment complex where the abuse grew very intense. On one occasion he accused me of dating someone I worked with and fought me for three days. He made me call out of work for those days and basically held me captive at knife point. This is when the real problem was revealed. He pulled a white substance out and snorted it up his nostrils, so this further let me know who I was dealing with. He kept telling me he was going to kill me on this particular day, but instead chose to stab me in my leg. I saw so much blood it scared me and apparently him too! I ran out the apartment screaming. He ran behind me acting as if it was an accident. He then rushed me to the hospital.

The abuse continued, but another life changing occasion happened. This time it was trauma to my left eye. He hit me so hard my eye blackened instantly! I went to the hospital again as I had done many times but always lied about what happened. My vision became blurry and continued to get worst. After several optometrist appointments, and months of being treated for something I didn't have, it was determined I had a retinal detachment caused by the blow I took to my eye. I had surgery, but it did not repair the damages.

During these encounters my family would find out and confront him, and even called the police several times. But, I would lie and say he didn't do anything to me. They didn't understand why I was defending him or why I wouldn't leave, but what they didn't know was he told me if I did decide to leave, he would kill my little sisters. I took the abuse thinking I'm saving my siblings. In my mind, if he was crazy enough to cause all the pain and affliction towards me, how far was he really willing to go?

Because my family didn't understand my reasoning, they told people I was on drugs, and I was not. It was hurtful to know people believed it, but because I was so frail it was believable but not true at all. The next traumatic experience I encountered happened because I was talking to a friend on the phone as he listened. She told me she talked to a supervisor she knew, and he would give me a job. He attacked me right after the call accusing me of being with the guy I never met. That night I was tied to a bed. He cut an extension cord from a lamp and left the plug in the socket. He started shocking me in my face until it was swollen almost beyond recognition; I stayed hidden for nearly a week.

As time went by more physical abuse happened, and I grew scared that one day I was going to be killed. One Sunday, a voice kept playing in my head saying if I didn't leave this would be the day I'd die. That day he was in and out of the house and would say he saw someone leaving each time. The difference this day was he didn't touch me, but his paranoia was high. The voice kept speaking to me this time saying, *"Run!"* I allowed him to leave again and after 15 minutes I ran as fast as I could, leaving everything.

I started my life over; it was a process. I thought I could never have kids, but after years I now have a loving husband, and three beautiful children. I went from being a high school drop-out to now holding an MBA and I work for one of the largest insurance firms. I have led many teams for many corporations. I am now telling my story, writing my book, and building platforms for others to do the same: "Outlive the Labels."

Shalonda Chaney-White

Shalonda Chaney-White is a newly discovered author, born and raised in Jackson, Tennessee. She has her master's degree in Business Administration with a concentration in Healthcare Management. She has managed multiple businesses and previous owned Shalonda's Succulent Taste Catering. She is currently a Complex Care Advisor for a multinational healthcare firm. She serves as a personal advisor and is working on certification as a life coach. She also served as a volunteer judge for a female solidarity association, during their 2021 local chapter scholarship program. She has three children whom she shares with her husband. She's currently launching a new book, joining the podcasting community, and has many more projects to come.

The Story of My Life

Rhonda Tatum

*T*he fall of 2013, I got into a situation where I risked my life. A friend told me about an opportunity to fix my credit if I participated in certain activities. At that time, I was in dire need of extra income to take care of my family. The gentleman in my life (who is also my children's father) wasn't doing his part as a partner for me or as a father. Headaches and 808 heartbreaks were a staple in that relationship to say the least. I was unemployed, but attending school to be a Massage Therapist/Physical Therapy Aide. The County building was my second home as I found myself there many days trying to keep some supplemental income coming in while attending school with no job. Anything that hinted at a speck of financial freedom, I was on board.

My friend and I started to confabulate about my life, and the hardships I was facing was the hot topic of our conversation. I stayed in San Bernardino, California and was on section 8. I had to do what was necessary to survive.

When an opportunity was presented to me, I hesitated until enough was enough. I was trying to live the easy life. I struggled paying bills and rent with no help. Having two children, I hustled in so many ways. Finally, I reached out to my friend. That's when the trial began. I was introduced to a guy named Mike who was already behind bars. Me, not thinking anything of it, I assumed he was behind bars for something normal and would get out soon. Nope! He convinced me that he could help me fix my credit; all I had to do was put a property in my name and they would fix the house and resell it. Man, it all sounded great because Mike told me he had done this plenty of times, and it worked out for everyone! I felt I had a chance to make money and improve my credit. Damn! This was awesome.

I followed along like a dummy and filled out the paperwork. I forged some things not realizing what I was doing was causing pain and hurt to me and my kids. All the transactions were through my bank and I split my money with someone else. In reality, it wasn't worth it. I'll never forget what happened next. It was September 2013. I received a call from my dude saying, "Hey, a detective came to the house looking for you!" Knowing his scary ass, he led the guy to me and lied to the detective about knowing about the situation. That's the kind of man he was. I called the detective back; his name was Mr. Black. I called Mike and panicked. Why is a detective trying to talk to me? "Just let them know you were dating Mr. Dan for four years, and he gave you the deed to the house," Mike said. With Mike's advice, I decided to return Mr. Black's call.

"Hi, is the Rhonda?" said Mr. Black.

"Yes, it is. How are you?" I said.

"I need to talk to you about some information I'm investigating."

My heart dropped! I paused and gave him my location. "I'm not in trouble or anything, right?"

He said I wasn't in trouble and met me at my school. I remember asking Mike before I got into this triangle, "Are you sure I'm not going to get into trouble?" Mike kept saying, "No! I know what I'm doing." Yeah right, that man had no clue how much trouble he put me in. Mr. Black showed up and I met him on the side of the building because I didn't want to be seen. It was so embarrassing talking to this man. You can tell something was up by the way he looked. I knew he was wired, but I didn't pay attention to that.

"I have a couple of questions," Mr. Black said.

"Okay," I responded.

"How do you know Dan?"

I told him everything Mike told me to say, but I messed up one thing. While talking to the detective, I told him about the tv show "Snapped" and how I recalled a scene where people were doing fraud. I told the detective, "I hope I don't end up like them one day." I would never think in a million years I would go to jail. In 2014, I graduated from school with a 4.0. I landed a job and got my life back on track. On November 4, 2014, I got a knock on the door. It was a powerful knock. *It's 7am; who is knocking on the door?* It was the San Bernardino Police. They asked if I was Rhonda and I responded, "Yes, why?" They had a warrant for my arrest and the bail was $365,000. My eyes got big! They gave me two choices: go with LAPD or sit in San Bernardino jail for two weeks.

Shaking my head, I went with the LAPD. I couldn't even shower that day. Can you imagine how I smelled? I cried and cried! I didn't understand why I was going through this. Walking through that jail, it was terrifying. I heard people yelling and screaming. I was fingerprinted and ended up in the county jail on 76th street in LA. I met different women who had all kinds of charges. I asked all kinds of questions. The DA didn't want to release me, but I'll explain later why it was best I stayed. I didn't take a shower for a week. I had to do blood work, eat horrible food, and sleep in cells with other women. I had no soap and couldn't brush my teeth for a week! The place had a horrible smell to it.

I found myself placed in the "yellows" – which meant mental housing. Why did I do that? Man, wrong idea! The first cellmate I ever had ate all the food I didn't eat and farted all night. The beds were hard to sleep on. You had only one blanket all night. If you used the bathroom, you had to go in front of cellmates. The walls were dirty; I couldn't even see out the window. It was like looking in a small mice hole. I had to get out of there! I met some trustees who worked in different housing sections in the jail. The two ladies helped me write a note to the counselors. I broke down so much I told myself this is my life until God says otherwise. I didn't blame God, I blamed myself.

My first court date was dreadful. I had to get up at 3:00am for the first two weeks. We were handcuffed side by side like killers and face the wall when other inmates walked by. I knew God had a plan for my life, but I didn't know the direction. Every night, I tossed and turned on those thin beds. I attended Bible studies and church weekly. The work kept me busy half the time. The other co-defendants were trying to go to trial and it pushed court dates longer, and made it hard for the DA to decide. I prayed Psalm 91 every day at the court for everyone who faced a judge. My mother couldn't afford my lawyer anymore, so I had to get a Public Defender. This was a blessing because she worked with this DA before. I remember going to court and meeting her for the first time. She told me about my charges. Not thinking, I said, "My last lawyer said he can get me six months to a year in the county jail." What a rude awakening! I was really looking at 14 years! Each charge was a year and by her not looking at the case yet and being AB109 (which means state body), the lawyer didn't even know my charge, time, or sentencing. I couldn't believe what I was hearing! "Maybe, I can get you four to six years," she said. "Lady, I can't do that, and I will not," I said with tears flowing.

I cried until I had no tears left. Each court date was unsuccessful. As time went on, I prayed. One day, a deputy came to me and said, "Your lawyer is here to speak to you." My heart was beating fast! It had been months and my lawyer couldn't give me an answer of sentencing or an offer from the DA. Before I walked to the phone, I was already praying and asking God to give me 16 months with half and claiming it for months now. When I got to the phone Mrs. Kim said, "I have good news for you." I was praying under my breath, *God please let it be 16 months with half.* Earlier, I mentioned that I was glad I stayed in jail. If I didn't serve all that time like I did, I would have had to go to jail in June 2015, and I wouldn't get out until February 2016. When I tell you God is so real, He is! I was super excited and happy. I finally knew I was going home! Two months later, I went to court and all charges were dropped except for two with no probation. I ended up going home two weeks later!

This message is for my readers. Please never doubt God and the plans He has for your life. It took this situation to happen in my life to sit me down. Don't take life for granted because I trusted people I shouldn't have trusted. There are battles in life and you must pick and choose your path. *Outlive the Labels* has changed me dramatically. I learned you do not have control over your life, GOD has the control. I was tested in so many ways; I didn't know how much longer I could hold on. I have changed my life and become someone greater.

Rhonda Tatum

Rhonda Tatum is a mother of two lovely children. She graduated from Chaffey High School before her class in 2004. Rhonda attended West Los Angeles College and graduated with an AA in Social and Behavioral Science. She started writing at the age 15 years old and always wanted to write a book about her life. Rhonda played sports and joined programs to help her enhance. Rhonda is currently a Certified Massage Therapist/Physical Therapy Aide. She's been in practice for 7.5 years and specializes in Deep Tissue Massage, Sport Massage, Swedish, CBD Massage, Hot Stone, Cupping and much more. She currently runs a Mobile Massage Therapy business traveling to client's homes to provide service. She sells CBD products, muscle balms, and body butters. She loves watching movies, listening to music, watching TV, writing, reading, working out and loves going out.

I See You
Laticka Weaver-Smith

I looked up at two familiar faces, that now seemed unfamiliar, through the blur of the tears that gathered in my eyes. My hands ached in pain. The bedroom seemed to spin. My fingers vibrated with this painful sensation. I looked up, unable to move my hands. He held them so tightly and high above my head. With so much pressure I could feel the force in my elbows and shoulders. My mouth was covered, a full breath was impossible. I could not breathe. I was suffocating. A multitude of tears streamed down my face, on both the left side and right side. I looked at the faces of people I knew. I hoped that they would see my tears and understand that they were hurting me. In desperation, I hoped that they would let me go. No, they did not notice. Their attention was on what was about to happen to me.

The room was silent except for the sound of the covers rustling beneath me as I tried to break free. My focus shifted downward. Then, I saw him coming towards me unbuckling his belt. He smiled at me as he came closer. This same boy I saw at my school in the primary classes. He is older than I am. Next, he loosened the top button and then the zipper of his pants. I began to kick. I wanted to scream, but I could not. "Y'all hold her; get her legs!" he said as he yelled orders to my family members. They adjusted in obedience to him. My cousin held one of my legs down at the knee. He was much older, taller, and bigger. I could not move. All I wanted to do was cry. Immediately, I felt helpless and everything stopped. I fell into a void of darkness. Everything stopped – there was nothing. I did not exist. Time didn't exist. I felt as if I were invisible, drunk, and sunken. I was empty.

Then suddenly I was let go. I jumped up and ran out of the room and they slammed the door behind me. I ran to the next door in the open floor plan apartment. I knocked on the door where the adult was. I banged on the door only to hear, "Stop knocking on my goddamn door!" She yelled through the door and didn't even bother to open it. I slumped down onto the floor, by her door, in the open space that shared the dining, living room, and kitchen. I pulled my knees to my chest and put my back against the wall. Now, time existed, everything existed and I cried. "Stop all dat noise!" she said again through the door. I sat there feeling totally and completely unseen. Hoping to be seen by her and that she would come out the door or at least open the door or something.

Praying that I did not get seen again by my family in the other room, I sat there and suddenly I had to pee. Now time, pain, fear, and tears existed. I shook as I sat by her door alone, knees pulled to my chest. Yes, I was tall for my age. Yes, I was big for my age. However, I was still my age. That wasn't the only time. This became a regular thing. So much so that they started taking turns. I hated going over to her house. Sometimes she would ask me to bring her some water and when I brought the water I would linger, hoping and praying that she wouldn't notice I was still in her room or kitchen. That way I wouldn't have to leave and go into the hallway. That's where it all started about thirty years ago.

Every abusive, neglectful, negative relationship started after that point. No one cared. No one wanted to hear or see me. Relationship after relationship got worse and worse. The abuse became more physical and then more mental. At one point I thought that I would lose my mind. Hell, I almost did during the ups and downs of abuse. I got married, graduated college, and gave birth to four wonderful, beautiful children. They became my strength to embark on something new and leave one bad relationship, hopefully, to start a new better relationship. Sadly, I was in a cycle. I repeated the same relationship and became that same little girl sitting in the hallway over and over again. I wore black eyes, bruises, and swollen neck, lips, and jaw regularly. When I called the police, I felt seen for a little while. The cops would come and forcefully make him leave. It gave me a little smirk to put on my face at that moment. What would I do? Bail him out, and let him come right back in.

One day there was a change in me. You see, time teaches lessons that only time can teach. Experience is the best teacher anyone can have. Sunday morning my children and I went to a service at Refuge Temple. My face was swollen from the punch I had received in the face the day before. It was swollen so bad that my cheek drooped down and my face resembled Two-Face from Batman. I took a picture of myself and sent it to his mother. In a desperate attempt to be seen; to be saved. I went to church without any attempt to cover my swollen face, black eye, or scratches on my neck. All in an attempt to be seen. I wanted someone to see me, see my suffering, and save me. To come in and stop all the pain, stop the misunderstanding, the abuse, and mistreatment. Yet no one did.

At church, it was a beautiful service. The Holy Ghost came through every pew from the pulpit to the door. We had an amazing time. I gathered my children together at the end of service and we began our walk home. When I unlocked and opened my front door, there he was. "Why'd you send them pictures to my mama?" he said furiously. No apologies for my face being swollen, no apologies for the scratches on my neck, or for the torn clothes that had to be thrown away. No, *I'm going to improve or try to do better*. No. Just *why you sent them pictures to my mama*? I said, "Simply, I wanted her to see what you do. This is what you do."

I walked through my home to avoid the argument. My children went upstairs to get undressed out of their church clothes. I continued through the foyer into my downstairs bathroom. He walked out the front door. I stood in my bathroom with my hands on the sink. I held onto that porcelain so tight I could have left my fingerprints in it. Standing there looking down at the faucet I realized that I had not looked in the mirror in years. At this moment I don't even know what I looked like. Why is it so hard for me to look up? Why is it so hard for me to see my reflection in this mirror? Why is it that I would much rather just look down right here at the sink? I've been in this bathroom thousands of times, brushed my teeth, and opened the medicine cabinet to get the toothpaste. All the while looking down at the drain. Never once looking up.

Today was different though. Today I understood and realized that I had not looked in the mirror. I slowly lifted my head and eyes from that drain to the faucet up to my mirror. And tears began to stream down my face. I saw that my face was swollen, most definitely my eye was black and blue and with red spots on the inside. There were four very deep scratches on the left side of my neck along with a few red bruises. I looked at myself, I looked in my eyes, and I said three words. Three words changed my life forever. No not, I love you. Not even words of encouragement like *you got this*, or faith-driven words like *God's got you.* Three simple words, the most important words to me. Words that I have been longing to hear. I *see* you. I said that to myself that day in the mirror. That same week I purchased *Act Like a Success, Think Like a Success* by Steve Harvey. I also purchased Dr. Daniel Amen's books on brain health.

I ended the repetitive cycle of abusive relationships. I created my first vision board. I truly began to see myself. I took the time to evaluate myself from where I was. I am still in the process of where I want to go. In 2009, I started the non-profit organization VisionNeed. Through VisionNeed I have helped many children from low-income areas (my neighborhood) go to college and I supported other programs in my area. I honestly feel that our future relies on the children and the desire to have their vision seen. I said on that day: Shenell, I see you.

Laticka Weaver-Smith

Laticka Weaver-Smith is a Mom, Entrepreneur, and CEO of Frank Services LLC, a local business named and dedicated after her great-grandfather Frank Weaver. Laticka is also the Founder of VisionNeed, a nonprofit organization dedicated to restoring hope in poverty-stricken communities through donations to programs such as the MRC, United Way, Big Homie Little Homie, and DJJ.

Redeemed and Delivered
Liliana Marie

*E*verything is labeled. For the most part they're useful. It's how you know you're opening a can of corn as opposed to a can of peas. Labeling people, however, is a different concept. Labels lead us to settle. They lead us to not work to our fullest potential and to others judging us on the package and not on what's inside – the content God gave us. The next thing I look for on my food packages are ingredients. To me that's an important factor. It took me a long time to look past my own label and look at what I was made of: the contents of my spirit, my soul, and the core of my very being. I was and always will be God's Daughter; made in the perfect likeness of His image. How can His image have a negative label? It cannot.

God had a calling on my life since I was a young girl. I knew there was something stirring inside of me. As a child I thought of being a Nun. I felt it deeply. I had empathy for those suffering, especially children. My parents took me to church on Good Friday and I'd weep uncontrollably at the death of Jesus; not even knowing who Jesus was. There were two roads available for me to take in order to walk into this calling. Mine and His. God gave me dreams of prison since a young teenager. Even though I wasn't saved then, He tried to warn me of the darkness that was looming if I were to go my own way. I was so concerned with changing my labels that I lost sight of who I was meant to be. There was a direction He wanted me to live and represent Him.

At the time, I already had labels from my family and my elementary school. I was trying to prove myself and outlive the labels on my own. I was in the "slow" track at school. My parents weren't happy with any accomplishments. The labels hurt and I needed a way out. However, I didn't understand that God's labels for me were Redeemed and Delivered. I went my own way even though I took the long road. There was no way to stop the amazing path that God had for me. God had a plan for my healing, and I chose a plan that would put me deeper into the miry clay. The encouraging part is, that even on my road to self-destruction, like Paul's road to Damascus God came and set me free. Unlike Paul, I wasn't persecuting others. I was persecuting myself. I'd bought into the lies that were spoken over my life. I felt rejected and inadequate.

I wanted to show my parents and family that I could be successful – that I could be someone they would be proud of. I wanted to show my elementary school that I wasn't slow. I was innovative and creative. I wanted to erase my own labels and change my identity without relying on Christ. I soon learned how wrong that was. I was a kind, young woman. I had a heart for others. I took care of younger children. I let wayward youth into my home. I gave my Christmas gifts away to children at the hospital, but on the inside I was broken by the weight of the labels. Because God is gracious and God is merciful, He erased my labels and gave me *Beauty for My Ashes,* but not until one final label was placed on my head: Felon!

My own way involved meeting some people on Craigslist who were supposed to make my dreams come true, but in retrospect led me to a four and one-half year sentence in a place of darkness and isolation. When I met them (still not saved) God spoke to my heart: *"Don't do it."* But, in my own quest of being labeled "successful and accomplished" I ignored the voice. God still loved me, and God still wanted me to fulfill my purpose. I had big hopes and dreams and wanted to change the world and leave my mark on it at the same time. I thought that if I could just do something amazing, that the bad labels would fall off and be replaced with "successful and "accomplished." What I succeeded in accomplishing was actually the opposite. The parents that I wanted so hard to impress lost their home and their business of 45 years and became homeless. We all became homeless. So much for changing that label without God.

I didn't look at who God said I was. I was too busy trying to please family and rid myself of the stigma. The wrong way. The wrong journey. It didn't matter because what God had for me was for me and no one could stop it including myself. As stated earlier, before incarceration, I was stripped of everything. My elderly parents and special needs son and I lost their million-dollar condo and their business thanks to my choices. We were left with nothing. I cried out to God and asked Him to spare me. In His own way He did. He led me to a church out of need but I walked out saved.

When I entered the prison gates six months later, I entered with Jesus and the Word implanted in my heart. I prayed for others fervently and with passion even though I had never prayed out loud before. I became versed in the Word. God gave me dreams and visions again. This time I knew they were from Him and I wanted nothing more than to be used by Him. My prayer changed from *"get me out"* to *"use me while I am here"* and He did. He moved me from prison to prison where I preached the Word of God and anointed bed posts and co-ran Bible studies and shed my own labels. Yes, I absolutely found deliverance. With deliverance came breakthrough. For me breakthrough was a process. It was a chiseling of old ways, habits, and thoughts. To date there are still some stubborn areas that God is working on.

I knew that the label of felon would linger and that many would use it against me. I also knew that God was on my side. From the inception of this incarceration, I dreamed a series of numbers 111. I began to see them in every interaction. It started my first night at Riker's when I dreamed the number. Then I went to commissary the next day and my bill was $111.11. Pages I opened to were 111. That number was the start of a number of prophetic messages that God gave me on my journey of helping others. This number as it turns out, became a catalyst in a miracle. I dreamed and saw the number for years. One day I was told that I would once again be changing locations, to a camp; the camp where I received my ultimate breakthrough.

Before leaving, I went to a church service as usual. One

of the church members pulled me to the side and whispered, "You don't belong here. But you're here for a reason. " It was nice to hear, but I had no idea that God was about to give me my new name. Until then I'd been an inmate number. But the labels were about to change. The labels were Loved, Chosen, Vessel of Honor, Amazing Grace. A few days after getting to the camp I met CC. CC was bunking with someone of another faith and God prompted me to speak to her and tell her the truth. God also prompted me to give CC my brand new Bible that I'd waited months to get. I'll be honest, I was hesitant with that one. I actually had the audacity to tell God no. It was my Kenneth Copeland Bible and I was looking forward to getting it in the mail. It wasn't even warm in my hands. I asked God for a fleece like Gideon. I said, *"God, if you really want me to give it to her she will walk past my cube"* and lo and behold she did! She cried and said she'd just written home for a Bible.

God continued to send me messages for CC; specific dates, in fact. At that time, I wasn't so bold, but God kept nudging me and often told me through dreams and the Word that if CC was obedient, she'd receive an immediate release. What I learned along this journey was to listen to God. The reason I was in this pit was because I had avoided His promptings. A week later CC told me her birthday was coming up. When I asked when it was, she said November 1st. Chills ran up my arm: 11/1! The number. God had been preparing me for this all along. I knew then that my labels were shed; that God had new names and new plans for my life! The ugly labels, the hurtful labels – those aren't the ones we own and they're the ones that we have to shed. God pursued me to pursue CC. He leaves the 99 for the one and she was the one!

> *"You need to persevere, so that after you have done the will of God, you will receive what He has promised. Patient endurance is what you need now, so that you will continue to do God's will."* Hebrews 10:36

❦

Liliana Marie

Liliana Marie is a job developer and mentor who helps mothers and daughters coming out of difficult situations find viable solutions to life's challenges while using her business skills to enhance confidence in these women and empower them to start their own cosmetics business as a means to self-sufficiency.

Before starting this work, Liliana worked a number of years as a resident aid and house manager. After a successful career as Founder and President of her own NPO, Liliana now trains and coaches young women in realizing their dream and potential. She is a certified life coach and certified in CBT, and is working towards a degree in youth ministry. Liliana loves writing, advocacy, and working with young children.

Liliana is available for your type of work or output and private consultations. You can reach her at 646-698-1656 and mentorandadvocate2020@outlook.com

The Pregnancy Story

Georgette Guess

*I*t was the week after he left. Suddenly, the sickness I was once feeling from what the radiologist defined as a "cyst" became more intense. That included discomfort and pressure to my pelvic area. I also experienced anything from minor headaches, dizziness, vomiting, and feeling extremely fatigue. My emotions were all over the place, and my heartbeat was rapid and strong. I began to weep. I was concerned and fear crept in. Reality was a slap in my face; I had marital issues that was left unresolved. So, how was I about to deal with this? I wanted answers and was determined to find out.

Of course, the first thing I did was take a pregnancy test. As I waited for the results of the test, several thoughts went through my mind such as, *"Could I really be pregnant?"* and *"If so, why now?"* My breathing became heavier; it was then that I realized I needed to relax. I started to overthink everything. The longer I waited my thoughts appeared deeper. Finally, the timer went off. That was the longest three minutes I have ever waited! My hand instantly started shaking and sweating; I was nervous to read the results. I took a deep breath, opened my eyes and lo and behold the test had determined I was pregnant. A part of me was excited because I thought a child with my husband would be a seal on our marriage and a gift to one another. In all this excitement, he wasn't there to take part in these steps and although I was angry, I humbled myself and called him hoping we could put the nonsense behind us and move forward.

The phone went straight to voicemail. I called back three other times and still no answer. Tears began to flow, yet again. Three months into our marriage and five days gone, why is this happening to me? Never did I imagine being in this place of brokenness. At this point I knew he was trying to hurt me by any means necessary, and if you ask me his decision was supported by people who should have held him accountable. He isolated himself from me as if I were a predator. I called and texted him, but he blocked me. I remember seeing him at church with his wedding ring off; I couldn't even look at him I was so disgusted by his blatant disrespect. As if things couldn't get any worse, he was sitting in a seat far away from me. I was humiliated and embarrassed that my children and the entire church witnessed this foolish behavior towards me. I was physically present, but my mind was elsewhere. All I wanted was the service to be over so I could leave. I must have walked into the bathroom at least a hundred times in that service. Each time I went, I cried and I cried some more; I couldn't understand how this man could be so cold hearted towards me.

Days turned into weeks; weeks turned into months

without a word from this man. I didn't know how to move forward; my heart was shattered with disbelief and broken promises. Somehow, I was grieving although he was alive. There were times when I felt I alone and misunderstood. My soul was in turmoil. I went through moments of depression where I couldn't get out the bed and when I laid down the tears soaked up the pillow. I remember with very little strength saying, "God, I need help."

Deeply wounded because I felt as if I was robbed of a gift that was supposed to be freely giving to me, I assumed everything about this would be a blessing. I was sadly mistaken because he didn't return home and made sure he deprived me of a joyful pregnancy. He wasn't there for anything: the maternity pictures, doctor's appointments, baby shower, labor and delivery. For months, I struggled with forgiving myself, feeling as if I betrayed me. Living in a place of deep regret, I was angry. I let my guard down and allow the same person to hurt me again. Truth be told, even after all that he put me through I wasn't ready to let him go because I still desired the marriage.

I was stuck in ruminating thought cycle, which was dangerous for my mental health and prolonged the depression. As I read an article from the American Psychological Association, and Nolen-Hoeksema said, "Many ruminators stay in their depressive rut because their negative outlook hurts their problem-solving ability." It wasn't until I started the journey of self-forgiveness and became intentional about my healing process that I looked up and the regret was gone! It was all because I was determined to overcome this obstacle and it immediately shifted my perception and I dealt with the inner critic. According to the Cambridge English Dictionary, the definition for victim is "to be hurt, damaged, or killed because of something or someone." Yes, at one point it did hurt, but the fact that I was still breathing was a clear indication that I was no longer a victim but a victor because I survived what could have killed me!

I want to encourage every woman who is pregnant to let go of self-sabotage, guilt, shame, and blame. You are more than enough and you're not responsible for who left. Please remember Romans 8:28 (NKJV) which declares, "And we know that all things work together for the good to those who love God, to those who are called according to His purpose." Enjoy your pregnancy sis!

❦

Georgette Guess

Georgette Guess wears many hats. She is a mother, life coach, evangelist, entrepreneur, author, and an anointed woman of God. Sadly, Georgette experienced tragedy early on in her life. At age eight, she was sexually assaulted. Her battle with this trauma created a yearning for true love and a lack of identity sent her on a path of self-destruction. Manifested hurt caused her to rebel against her mother and misbehaved in school. At the age of fifteen, she became a mother. The suddenness of parenthood motivated her to go after her destiny.

Georgette soon obtained her high school diploma, and later attended Paul Mitchell Cosmetology School where she received her cosmetology license. Georgette is the owner of Royalty Kids Learning Center, LLC and the former owner of Salon Royalty, LLC. Georgette has been featured in EntreprenHer Magazine as one of the Top 50 Inspirational Woman in the Country. She also holds a bachelor's degree in Theology. She is the visionary of Her Story Initiative, Inc., which is a sisterhood for adolescent and adult women. The Her Story Initiative offers companionship, counseling, and inspiration for survivors. Her rise from tragedy transformed into a mission to support and uplift her community. She continues to stand in the gap for others who are survivors of tremendous trauma to help them receive their deliverance through the Lord.

Her favorite scripture is Luke 1:45, *"Blessed is she who has believed that the Lord would fulfill his promises to her!"*

The Metamorphosis of Beginning
Amber Keys

"*There is no way you're making it out of this, throw in the towel now,*" a voice demanded. I sat on the floor in my living room with my four-month pregnant belly, tears falling down my face. I wept, inhaling and exhaling deeply. I listened to that voice; it made sense as to why I should quit. My heart began to palpitate, and the tears kept flowing. The voice grew louder, and now appeared to have grown legs, feet, arms, hands, a full body. It felt as if it sat right next to me with the towel on a silver platter to serve-defeat.

There was a song playing by Todd Galberth called "Lord You Are Good." I had it on repeat, but my tears were too loud to hear the words, my cry had shaken the room. I heard the melody play softly in my ears, I adhered to the tune, next came the words. He said in the song "*...You've been so good...so many times you healed me...*" He said it a few times and each time I listened more intensely as I lifted my head. I thought about the many times before this very moment that God has been there for me. I now cried out in total gratitude. I then heard the words *"…I had to declare from a hard place that you still been better…when I almost lost my mind…"* I screamed.

The words "I had to declare from a hard place" is what took root in my soul and spirit. It registered greatly because I was in my hard place. I was in that place declaring that God has *still* been better than good. It was a prophetic declaration to my hard place. Announcing it will not hold me long. It was a declaration of remembrance to shift my mind to understand this hard place is truly, temporal. It was in that moment that I got my breakthrough. I was liberated into another place both spiritually and mentally.

"Sometimes, the breakdown is needed, for the breakthrough…don't give up"- Roxana Jones. Breakdown is what gives way to the breakthrough.

The term breakdown by Webster Dictionary states, "Failure to progress or have effect," or "The process of decomposing." Life at times can cause crippling, strife, and turmoil. "And he said unto me, My grace is sufficient for thee: for my strength is made perfect in weakness. Most gladly therefore will I rather glory in my infirmities, that the power of Christ may rest upon me." 2 Corinthians 12:9 (KJV) I find this scripture comforting. It is reassurance in my *hard place* that when my strength fails, his strength is made perfect in me. The perfect strength of God beholds all elements of that which is complete—it is free from faults and imperfections. It exists in moments of breakdown because the resolve is the sum total of perfect strength to ensure your triumph.

What is important to understand is that in breakdown

it is not only a process, but a time where you will see yourself in every form of your naked truth. However, in this moment what is equally important, is, the power to surrender. What are you surrendering to exactly? The great shedding of the old. It never feels good, but what emerges from the shedding is always much more beautiful. You must find your sound in breakdown and follow that sound. There is a sound in breakdown that proceeds breakthrough. There is a sound of acceptance that births contentment. Follow the sound in breakdown, there is a melody called breakthrough to follow.

The definition of breakthrough is "act or instance of moving through or beyond an obstacle." Obstacles come by way of life challenges and often out of your control. However, the joy is, there is something worthy on the other side of that obstacle. You must hold on through the breaking to see what will be produced. Breakthrough requires a breaking, there would be no need for a breakthrough if there wasn't anything that needed to break. Now there are moments where you may not feel a breaking is necessary, but there is always a better version of you to emerge. You will not meet him/her without deconstruction of who you are currently.

Many people like to skip the molding and would rather be the shiny piece put on display; forgetting—those shiny pieces are shallow, and they are just what they are, a display. You want to be the masterpiece—that takes times and development. The masterpiece will always have a longer shelf life than a display, in value and aesthetics. Remember displays are toyed with, tossed around, and used. A masterpiece is looked upon as high value, handled with care or cannot be touched at all.

When your breakthrough happens, you have now shifted into another paradigm. Breakthrough is what happens beyond the break. This shift has taught you many lessons, this shift has healed you, this shift has reset your mental default settings. This shift has allowed you to draw closer to God, this shift has changed your perspective, this shift has caused a release. As a result of the release, your becoming has taken form.

For those wondering, let me help you: *who qualifies for a breakthrough?* Everyone who is becoming. *What is a breakthrough and what are the components?* A breakthrough is what sets your future in motion as a result of the changes happening in your present. The components of a breakthrough are: the breakdown, the shedding, and the healing. The *breakdown* is what introduces you to yourself in a more profound way. You meet yourself at ultimate brokenness. Then comes the *shedding* of that which has caused the brokenness to begin with. It is the shedding of unforgiveness, poor decisions, sorrow, shame, defeat etc.

Lastly, the *healing*. This is the part where you get to meet the new you, the new you that took on a new form and identity. The healing is not without pain, but it is a pain that causes you to thirst for breakthrough and seek after it. The healing is what ushers in a peace in the process of it all. Here's a tip, pull strength from those who have already healed from their brokenness/processes, thus experienced their breakthrough. *When will it come?* Every individual's set appointed time differs. But everyone's breakthrough comes at the appointed time. Your appointed time may come in two months and someone else's appointed time may come in six months. However, rest in the fact that it *will* come. Breakdown is temporal. So, learn, feel and grow in the moment and season of breakdown.

Breakdown is nothing more than a posture that calls your breakthrough near. *Where does it come from?* Breakthrough comes from a deep embedded place within that is directly connected to a supernatural power source that is greater than anything we can fully comprehend. It is a place that houses an extra reservoir of strength. We do not use it until its designated time. *Why does a person need a breakthrough?* It serves as a force, a change agent that calls you into your destined place. *How can an individual get a breakthrough?* 1) Embracing the components of it, (talked about above) 2) Faith. Faith is what causes us to believe. To have faith in something you cannot see is what gives life to that very thing. Faith will set the tone that you know it can and will happen for you. It is the engine that drives each component of the breakthrough. Guess what? You do not need a lot, start with a mustard seed of it; it can move mountains.

Breakthrough is an expected end following a beautiful beginning.

❧

Amber Keys

Amber Keys is a native of Connecticut and a mom of three boys. She is the founder of Abundant Journey University and Crown'd Allure, LLC. She has earned her A.S. degree in Human Services and certificate in Youth Work/Human Services from Gateway Community College. She has years of serving and assisting people in multiple capacities. She sits on the board as Vice President for I Am Woman, LLC. She has served doing outreach in the community, local events and youth group homes.

Amber found her passion early on, she discovered her gift of helps at nine years of age. She knew she wanted to be someone great who made an impact. As the third oldest of 11 siblings, growing up Amber wanted to be role model for her younger siblings. In fact, that is where it all started for her. Home.

Her love for God and writing is what helped her not only navigate through her own life challenges, but discover her purpose. Amber found her voice and her audience and paired that with hunger to see change. She paired that with her desire to help others along their journey, become. Her passion is to inspire people of all walks of life to become their highest and most authentic version of themselves in every aspect. As a believer, transformational coach, and purpose influencer she takes pride in using her gifts to help people in the community. She is most passionate in assisting individuals as they undergo the stages of growth, giving them the tools to navigate and pivot. She is a writer, speaker, humanitarian, educator, and agent of change. People who come in contact with her presence will leave liberated.

www.ingramcontent.com/pod-product-compliance
Lightning Source LLC
Chambersburg PA
CBHW070053100426
42740CB00013B/2836